New Gardens in
PROVENCE
30 CONTEMPORARY CREATIONS

Editor: Jennifer Eiss
Translator: Louisa Jones
Designer: Séverine Morizet

Library of Congress Cataloging-in-Publication Data is on file with the Library of Congress.

ISBN-13: 978-1-58479-545-Z
ISBN-10: 1-58479-545-X

Published in 2006 by Stewart, Tabori & Chang
An imprint of Harry N. Abrams, Inc.

The text of this book was composed in Helvetica Neue and Suburban

Printed and bound in Spain
10 9 8 7 6 5 4 3 2 1

HNA
harry n. abrams, inc.
a subsidiary of La Martinière Groupe

115 West 18th Street
New York, NY 10011
www.hnabooks.com

LOUISA JONES   *Photographs by Bruno Suet*

New Gardens in
PROVENCE

30 CONTEMPORARY CREATIONS

Contents

Introduction
Gardens in Provence: Yesterday, Today, and Tomorrow   6

Small Secret Gardens   11

1/30 Rustic Revisited
A Mountain Village Courtyard   14

2/30 Taking a Break
A City Office Garden   20

3/30 Family Plots
In a Var Suburb   26

4/30 Sculpture in Camera
A Restaurant Garden in Monaco   34

5/30 Land Art, Japanese Style
A Farm with a View in the Luberon   40

Story Telling   49

6/30 Virtuoso Variations
The Domino Courtyards of Pierre Bergé   52

7/30 Old-fashioned Country Living
A Bastide in the Alpilles   60

8/30 Natural Exoticism by the Sea
A Golden Villa in the Var   66

9/30 Cliff Hanging
An Eagle's Nest in the Luberon   74

10/30 A Giant Riviera Rockery
A Seafront Villa Near Cannes   84

Wild and Woodland Gardening   95

11/30 Ancient Landscapes
A Wine Estate in the Alpilles   98

12/30 Contemporary Picturesque
Seafront Cliffs Near Marseille   104

13/30 Working Woodland
An Eighteenth-Century Domain Near Aix   110

14/30 Horticultural "High Tech"
An Architect's Retreat in the Var   118

15/30 Romantic Exoticism
A Town Emporium at L'Isle-sur-la-Sorgue   124

Sculpted Landscapes   133

16/30 Living in the Woods
A Contemporary House Near Uzès   136

17/30 Agricultural Land Art
An Old Farmstead in the Alpilles   144

18/30 Japanese Miniature
In a Mountain Château Park   152

19/30 Symbolic Quests
The Alchemist's Gardens and the
Noria Gardens   158

20/30 A Giant Chessboard
A "Folly" in the Gard   166

V Stone Lines   175

21/30 Gentle Minimalism
An Olive Orchard Near Grasse   178

22/30 Hillside Geometries
A Mountain Winery   188

23/30 Marine Terraces
An Admiral's Perch Near Toulon   194

24/30 Picturesque Formalism
Woodland Walls in the Luberon   202

25/30 Sculpture and Horticulture
A Photographer's Holiday Home   212

Community Sharing   221

26/30 Mandarin's Delight
A Bamboo Nursery Near Grasse   224

27/30 A Town for Tomorrow
Graveson, Village in the Alpilles   232

28/30 A Painter's Vision Renewed
Botanical Collections in the Var   240

29/30 Allotment Gardening
The "Castellas" in Marseille   250

30/30 Ambulo, Ergo Sum . . .
Andy Goldsworthy at Digne   256

Addresses
for Gardens and Landscapes in Provence   265

Introduction

Gardens in Provence: Yesterday, Today, and Tomorrow

Provence today is a hive of garden activity. Top international designers, local stars, home gardeners, nursery owners, and community organizers are all busy making gardens. Plant fairs and garden clubs have sprung up all over the region. Well-established traditions are once again adapting to global influence—something Provence has been doing since the Greeks first settled here in 600 B.C. Such vibrant growth, though not without risks, is a delight to behold.

I began visiting gardens in Provence in the 1970s. People said then that there were *no* gardens here, apart from certain famous historic properties near Aix and on the Riviera. I gradually understood that they were thinking of English flower gardens designed for summer display, a model foreign to both the climate and customs of Mediterranean France. The northern version is also purely ornamental,

and hides everything utilitarian from view. But the Roman heritage, still predominant in the south, never made this separation between productive and pleasure gardening. And when fruit counts as much as flower, every season has its attractions. Today the Mediterranean way of life has become fashionable worldwide. The symbol of its success is the olive tree, worshipped—perhaps even too much at times—for both its oil and its year-round beauty. Thanks to its legendary longevity, it embodies both landscape memory and future promise.

For my first books, *Gardens in Provence* and *Gardens of the French Riviera*,[1] I visited some 300 gardens between Nîmes and Menton, of all kinds and from all periods. Coupled with studies in local history, this investigation led me to articulate the differences between north and south. In those

days, Provence was still a sleepy backwater of the garden world, and my first book helped many southerners take pride in their own traditions. Now, decades later, Provence's best gardens—like its cuisine—rank with the finest international examples. Both blend global trends with a regional character now widely recognized and appreciated. Architect Hugues Bosc comments: "Gardens today have become an integral part of contemporary living in Provence.[2] Only ten years ago, people settling in the region first approached an architect and a decorator. The garden came last, and few designers were available. Since then, priorities have changed radically. The architect and the garden designer come first." More recently still, the garden-maker works with or is a visual artist. The "art of living" has evolved toward Art.

Geographically, the focus is also shifting: wealthy cosmopolitans are leaving the Riviera for western Provence. Drawn first by the unspoiled landscapes of the Luberon and the Alpilles, they are now spreading to more remote parts like the Var, the Mont Ventoux and the Gard. All of these areas draw internationally famous garden designers. Should their work for a privileged elite, here or elsewhere, be discounted because of the budgets involved? Why do we accept that architects like Le Corbusier fund their innovations by working for wealthy clients, but scoff at the same situation in the garden world? Enlightened private patronage has helped put Provence in the forefront of global design today.

Besides, today's garden mania affects everyone. New schools have been founded, catering to both career specialists and home gardeners. Old aristocratic families are transforming their estates into botanic gardens, beautifully arranged orchards, or outdoor museums. Modest grandmothers continue to exchange their cuttings, and some are now giving classes in traditional cooking and gardening. Small-budget efforts may be just as original and noteworthy as designer work. Several examples are presented in this book.

Young professionals today are often of the hands-on variety, refusing to accept an older generation's separation between conceptualization and groundwork. They have become "gardenists."[3] As ethnologist Françoise Dubost puts it so well, "to create with your hands, you also need your head."[4] What impresses me most in the current garden scene in Provence is the number of talented young people who are devoting their lives to garden and landscape care, inspired by a love of nature and ecological idealism.

Garden and Landscape

A garden can be almost anything: story, picture, architecture, sculpture; a conceptual game with form and space or a material, sensuous experience; a wildlife reserve, nature trail, philosophical exercise, scientific laboratory or ecological manifesto; an affirmation of identity—individual or community; a private refuge or an expression of group solidarity. Two main developments have occurred in France in recent years: the recognition of garden-making as a fine art, and the affirmation of its links with ecology. Far from being contradictory, these two modes blend over and over again, often with inspiring results. In Provence, a new Land Art has emerged from ancient practices such as the mixing of sculpted stone and clipped greenery, geometrical field patterning and dry-stone terracing (see chapters IV and V). All these experiments play on exchanges between garden and landscape.

These terms mean different things to different people. A botanist tells me that Les Colombières, created by the artist Ferdinand Bac in Menton in the 1920s, is not a garden but a landscape. Others consider it one of the first great landscape gardens, an inspiration to designers worldwide, including Mexican architect Luis Barragan. A young southern French designer, Sandrine Cnudde, explains about one of her own works: "I find it hard to call it a garden because its edge is like a fringe." John Dixon Hunt, British garden historian, proposes three categories: First Nature (or wilderness), Second Nature (cultivated land), and Third Nature, (the garden). He also suggests that landscape corresponds to prose, while gardens are like poetry.[5] French theorists object that "landscape" is really a mental construct deriving from cultural bias rather than actual topography, which they call "environment."[6] In eighteenth-century Europe, only the elite saw countryside as "landscape."[7] A hundred years later, when Cézanne first painted the Mont Saint Victoire, local farmers still had no interest in fine views. Only in recent decades has aesthetic appreciation for landscape touched everyone, city dweller and shepherd alike. Now, of course, views have serious commercial value—though we do not always protect them as we might. Nonetheless, lovers of rural France today often experience its landscapes as vast gardens.

Another key word today is "site." Designers everywhere talk about "spirit of place" and claim to be "site-oriented." This usually means they use existing elements in any proposed location to enhance its unique character. New owners once took possession by tearing up everything, even mature trees, but today they tend to respect vestiges of former land use. Some still import water to impose unlikely greenswards, but "waterwise gardening," where site-compatible ground covers replace grass, is making headway. Expensive lawns are often attributed to cosmopolitan residents, not always fairly. In fact, foreign gardeners have sometimes drawn locals' attention to the beauty of drought-resistant "weeds," like cistus or acanthus. Newcomers have certainly helped awaken today's widespread interest in plant diversity, both horticultural and natural.

Site-adapted, native plantings are often associated with "wild" gardening. This term also means many things: leaving nature to its own devices, protecting it, imitating it or integrating it into the garden, all approaches which again blur distinctions between garden and landscape. Once more, our vision changes as well as our plantings. When the fashion for wildflower meadows spread in northern Europe, southerners cast a fresh eye at their abandoned pasturelands, so full of spontaneous bloom in spring. Wild gardening is not simple in Provence however—owners complain that their newfound harmony with nature is disrupted on the one hand by hunters and on the other by wild boar, for whom the immediate solution seems to be . . . hunters.

Gardens always relate to the landscape outside, whether to reject, concentrate, embrace, or imitate it. Traditionally, few Provençal gardens are completely enclosed, and most enjoy continuity with the world outside. The agricultural connection is the most ancient, dating back at least to Roman villas. Country estates sit amidst their fields like the yolk of an egg. Plantings close to the building protect it from wind, help water to circulate, admit winter sun but provide summer shade. The formalism of evergreen hedges and parterres

echoes the geometries of surrounding vineyards, orchards, and wheat fields. The Romans called such productive landscapes *agri*, and the first serious contemporary gardens made in western Provence some thirty years ago emulated this model.[8] More recently, gardeners have taken inspiration from ancient village sites that rise in layers on hilltops. These are dry gray and silver gardens where stone counts as much as plants—tough subshrubs such as rosemary, lavender, etc. This kind of untilled, rocky, uneven landscape was used for pastures, hunting, and foraging. It was called the *saltus* by the Romans and is known as *garrigue* or *maquis* today. *Agri* and *saltus* are still very much with us today, but a third element has also come to the fore: the *silva* (wooded hillside). Often this is abandoned farmland evolving toward new-growth forest. The *silva* lends itself more readily than the *ager* or *saltus* to the adaptation of Picturesque and Romantic modes, encouraging what is almost a cult for trees. The *silva* also provides a fertile meeting ground for ecological experimentation with the new Land Art.

The Picturesque dotes on idealized images of untamed nature (see chapter III). Adepts, now as in the eighteenth century, spare no effort or expense to create an impression of spontaneity. Visitors may say, like the hero of Rousseau's novel *Julie, ou, la Nouvelle Héloïse*, "This place is enchanting, it is true, but rustic and wild; I see no human labor here." Today, as then, the gardener may answer: "It is true . . . that nature did it all but under my direction, and there is nothing here

that I have not designed."[9] This is one type of "natural" gardening. Another, the marriage of ecology and Land Art, works from a completely different premise: Instead of hiding human intervention, it puts it on show. Artistic creation is considered part of the species definition of *Homo sapiens*. The Land Artist is therefore neither dominant nor self-effacing but an active participant in an ongoing ecosystem (see chapters IV and V). The Picturesque and the ecological approaches are philosophical opposites, but both marry the garden to its site. Many owners interviewed for this book said proudly, "It looks as if it has always been there, don't you think?" This is a new ambition for gardeners in Provence.

A Humanist Ideal

How we situate ourselves in nature is revealed by the way we link house, garden, and landscape. The currently fashionable Mediterranean lifestyle supposes a harmony among all three, a nostalgic, idealized image of country life often focused on the *bastide* (country estate). This term has been subject to much commercial vulgarization, but when such old properties undergo sensitive restoration, their blending of use and beauty can be easily and elegantly adapted to contemporary needs. Bruno Lafourcade, an expert in the genre, explains his views: "For me, true minimalism consists in reinstating the mood of houses as they used to be, with whitewashed walls, simple stone or tile floors, beautiful materials with a minimum of furniture. Such an interior can hide today the most advanced technology."[10]

Houses built in a contemporary minimalist style are also proliferating in Provence, where they are often set off by "wild" or "natural" gardens. Contrast can be striking between sleek, simple buildings and intricate, multiform growth. Other parts of the world seek different effects—Californians may surround such houses with agaves and cacti to reinforce architectural formalism. Or again, in places where genuine wilderness survives or where it has been artificially recreated (as in the Netherlands), designers of "wild" gardens hide the house from view altogether or disguise it, along with the paths, as embarrassing evidence of human intrusion. In the Mediterranean world, where landscapes have been humanized for millennia, wilderness does not exist except, perhaps, in the Alps. Even the new Picturesque, southern style cheerfully displays vineyards and olive groves—human activity—with its woodland (see chapter III).

The Provençal juxtaposition of minimalist architecture with wild settings bears witness both to this ancient Mediterranean partnership and to its reinterpretation in today's ecological Land Art. The latter accepts that *Homo sapiens*, like other species, must invest its territory with habitats and trails. Thus, paradoxically, as ecological gardening gains favor, architecture plays a greater role. One significant difference from past centuries, however, is that houses participate but no longer dominate. Even in restored historic properties where the building remains central, the park's layout is no longer experienced merely as an extension of its architecture. And when house

and garden are made at the same time, there can be enthusiastic collaboration between garden-makers and such architects as Jean-Michel Wilmotte, Philippe Starck, Marc Barani, Maurice Sauzet, Rick Mather, or François Privat (to name only those encountered in preparing this book). This dialogue goes well beyond simple juxtaposition to promote subtle interactions between dwelling and setting. The garden assimilates human habitat into natural process. Culture and nature are experienced as versions of each other, not in opposition.

The human presence in Provence has not always been salutary for the rest of the biosphere, far from it. There exists, however, an ancient tradition of partnership. Le Corbusier, at the end of his life, admired the ancient Mediterranean hilltowns anchored to their site but also "looking toward the infinite horizon."[11] Historians of Mediterranean landscapes always stress "the perfect integration of the traditional rural house into its surroundings," and Jean-Robert Pitte even adds, "The term 'mimicry' is not too strong."[12] Jean Cabanel, founder of the French *Mission du Paysage*, concludes, "The vision of the Alpilles, where mankind is omnipresent, fills me with admiration. The smallest patch or field, the line of a furrow, the curve of a country lane, the drystone walls, all of these are the result of some thoughtful human gesture made in harmony with the place."[13] This age-old Mediterranean alliance is inspiring today's garden-makers to a new, creative participation in a natural process.

Notes : [1] Gardens in Provence *(Flammarion, 1992)* and Gardens of the French Riviera *(Flammarion, 1994). Both appeared in soft cover in 2000.* [2] *Hugues Bosc and Michel Semini,* De pierre et de nature *(private publication, 2003).* [3] *See the address list at the back for more details.* [4] *Françoise Dubost,* Les Jardens ordinaires *(L'Harmattan, 1997), p. 165.* [5] *John Dixon Hunt,* Greater Perfections: The Practice of Garden Theory *(Thames and Hudson 2000).* [6] *For example, Augustin Berque,* Les Raisons du paysage de la Chine antique aux environnements de synthèse *(Hazan, 1995).* [7] *Hunt develops this aspect in his book* The Picturesque Garden in Europe *(Thames & Hudson, 2003).* [8] *See Michel Racine,* Jardins de Provence *(Édisud-Arpej, 1987). The first famous contemporary example was the Jas Créma in northern Provence, followed by the Petit Fontanille, Val Joanis, and others.* [9] *Jean-Jacques Rousseau,* Julie, or, the New Heloise, *transl. by Philip Stewart and Jean Vaché, University Press of New England, 1997, p. 388.* [10] *Interview notes recorded in preparation for a private publication,* Lafourcade: restaurations, constructions, créations *(2003).* [11] *Most of the historians quoted here describe only Le Corbusier's Villa Savoye, the house near Paris that floats on stilts above an undeveloped pasture. William J. R. Curtis, in his book* Le Corbusier: Ideas and Forms *(Phaidon, 1986), goes deeper into the evolution of the architect in his attachment to Mediterranean sites. In the unfinished "Roq et Rob" project, Le Corbusier took inspiration from southern medieval hilltowns. Curtis considers that "this was 'regionalism' at its best: combining old and new, responding to climate, site, vegetation, views and local precedent." (Page 168.)* [12] *Jean-Robert Pitte,* Histoire du paysage français, *volume I (Tallandier, 1986), p. 141.* [13] *Jean Cabanel,* Paysage. Paysages *(Jean-Pierre de Monza, 1995), p. 45.*

Small secret gardens

Mediterranean courtyards have functioned as outdoor rooms since Roman times, long before the Californian version by Thomas Church[14] or the British adaptation by John Brookes.[15] In Provence, houses with enough land often have patios on all sides to allow for outdoor living at every time of day, in all seasons. One "outdoor room" in a medieval hilltown even solved a lawsuit that occurred when the entire terrace of a village house fell into a ravine after a huge storm. The property had been sold *en viager*, a system that allows sellers to remain in residence until their demise. Were the buyers responsible for expensive repairs even though they did not yet live on the site? Insurance companies demurred until it was judged that this terrace constituted an outdoor room of the house, necessary for entertaining friends. Thus defined, it was eligible for compensation!

Outdoor rooms in Provence exist in great variety, including courtyards in eighteenth-century townhouses, office gardens for working people, and restaurant terraces. Garden designer Michel Semini specializes in hidden village courtyards remodeled for stars of the film and fashion worlds, hideaways that allow celebrities to enjoy a weekend retreat without too much upkeep. Quite another type of small garden is the southern version of the British cottage style, though there was never an enclosure law in Provence that produced a cottage culture as such. The Mediterranean equivalent is called the "grandmother's garden" and is very much alive today.[16]

Parisian writers sometimes define the garden as a space that is limited, private, and enclosed, as opposed to landscape, which is boundless, open, and public. But these criteria are not universal. In residential neighborhoods, a broad stretch of lawn links one house to the next in a seemingly endless sea of green. American landscape architect Peter Walker went so far as to imagine a "minimalist garden

without walls,"[17] held together by its internal coherence in the manner of a painting without a frame. The opposition of enclosed garden and open landscape also breaks down in the Mediterranean world. Even small courtyards are rarely cut off entirely from their surroundings and often have a view. There, as in open countryside where fields are bordered with cypress hedging on one side only, it is climate that determines closure—open to the south, closed north against the fierce mistral wind. The uneven terrain of Provence complicates conventional definitions even further, as is beautifully illustrated by this idyllic small garden described by the novelist Henri Bosco: "Nestled under the terrace, protected by high stone walls that retain the warmth of the sun, it lay open to the valley beyond, with its blue and brown hilltops, offering to its roses, tulips, honeysuckle and even to its weeds warm bursts of air scented with fruit, hawthorn, and hyssop. Birds chirped among the plums . . . nothing could be more charming than this garden. It offered up this tiny, sheltered space to mankind, below the great benevolent house."[18]

Terraced hillsides like this one, protected and panoramic all at once, suit small gardens admirably. One of the best in Provence in recent years is La Louve, a hilltown garden made on three levels by Nicole de Vésian.[19] A former fashion designer, she restored her house for best views onto the garden, then planted the latter to set off the surrounding landscapes. This continuity is reinforced by plant choices, since the green and gray globes near the house are often made from the very plants that grow, unclipped, on the opposite hillside: holly oaks, juniper, arbutus, viburnum, rosemary, etc. There is no boundary here but a modulated series of planes, moving from house to garden to landscape, from the clipped to the wild, from intimacy to infinity.

Even a completely enclosed courtyard can "bring in the country" in various ways. The tops of neighboring trees, or nearby mountaintops, may add a strong presence beyond the wall. But perhaps the connection remains in the mind's eye only. Ever since the Romans painted optical illusions on their courtyard walls, designers have been using this technique to make small spaces seem bigger. A clever management of levels, of certain colors, of vertical plantings, of mirrors, of pots that are moved from place to place according to shifting sun and shade—all these can affect the perception of volumes.[20] Noel Kingsbury, a British designer specializing in naturalistic plantings, stresses a necessary balance between complexity and coherence, readability and mystery, while suggesting techniques that will allow the smallest garden, even in the heart of a city, to serve as a wildlife refuge. But there are also designers who deliberately blur readability, particularly of scale, in small enclosed spaces. The resulting disorientation, reinforced by exotic symbols, is an invitation to imaginary voyages.

Asian gardens, often tiny, have for millennia represented outside landscapes through symbolic miniaturization—a small fountain symbolizes a great river. Sir Roy Strong, author of several books on small gardens, considers that too many statues in a limited

space make it look like a cemetery.[21] In Provence, one would think rather of a flea market! But Marc Nucera, a tree sculptor working mainly on landscape specimens, has organized in his tiny courtyard a series of arrangements which evoke *garigue* scenes with just a dead tree branch, a stone, and a carefully pruned box plant in a pot. A dozen such scenes, each unique but all echoes of each other, deck his high walls. These are not bonsais but miniature landscapes, each carefully situated with respect to its place-ment and its fellows. The result is perfectly harmonious. Internal coherence suffices to delimit each scene.

For historian Helen Leach, "the outdoor living room/garden is an exercise in boundary definition, just as much as the wild marginal garden at the opposite end of the spectrum."[22] Perhaps all gardens, whatever their size, are both closed and open, retreats and quests . . . .

Notes : [14] *Thomas D. Church,* Gardens Are for People *(University of California Press, 1995).* [15] *John Brookes,* Room Outside *(Studio Books, 1970). Brookes has published a number of intelligent, practical books on home gardening, evolving recently toward landscape gardening.* [16] *See a book by Nicole Arboireau,* Jardins de grands-mères *(Édisud, 1998).* [17] *Peter Walker and Cathy Deino Blake, "Minimalist Gardens without Walls," in* The Meaning of Gardens, *ed. Mark Francis and Randolph T. Hester, Jr. (MIT Press, 1991), pp. 120–130. See also Paul Cooper,* Gardens without Boudaries *(Mitchell Beazley, 2003).* [18] *Henri Bosco,* Le Trestoulas *(Gallimard, Collection Folio, 1979), p. 17.* [19] *For more information on the garden of Nicole de Vésian, see Louisa Jones,* Gardens of Provence *(Flammarion, 1992) and* The French Country Garden *(Thames &Hudson, 2000).* [20] *Noel Kingsbury,* Natural Gardening in Small Spaces *(Frances Lincoln, 2003).* [21] *Roy Strong,* Creating Small Gardens *(Sterling Publishing, 2000).* [22] *Helen Leach,* Walled Pleasure Gardens and Outdoor Rooms," *in* Cultivating Myths: Fiction, Fact and Fashion in Garden History *(Godwit Publishing, 2000), p. 140.*

Left page top:
An "outdoor room," created by John Brookes.

Middle:
The courtyard garden made for a French film star by Michel Semini.

Lower:
The garden of a Provençal grandmother, the *Mère veilleuse*.

Above:
A miniature symbolic landscape in the courtyard of Marc Nucera.

Opposite above:
The patio of English garden designer and author Alex Dingwall-Mayne.

Below:
Detail of the famous garden by Nicole de Vésian that links intimacy and infinity.

Rustic Revisited

A Mountain Village Courtyard

Area: Southern courtyard, less than 2,000 square feet; north courtyard, 170 square feet.
Designer: Michael van Gessel (landscape architect).
Begun about 1990.

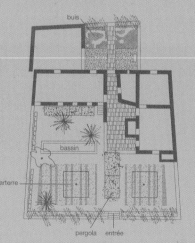

In 1984, three friends on vacation in northern Provence fell in love with a village house that had been abandoned for over thirty years. One was Dutch landscape architect Michael van Gessel, former participant in the famous international garden festival at Chaumont-sur-Loire. Restoration of the tiny courtyards naturally fell to him. The owners of this property have the right to draw water from the village fountain just outside the gate one afternoon a week—the designer therefore started by installing a buried cistern for water storage.

Opposite:
The clean lines of the pool and parallel rows of box echo the trunk of
the linden tree. Beyond the wall is
the village church.

Above left:
Steps lead to the back courtyard.

Middle:
In the back, roses rise from the
box nursery bed that van Gessel
calls "a sort of knotted maze
like a dreamy sea, or voluptuous
serpentine."

Right:
The main axis. On the pergola is a
"Muscat de Hambourg" grapevine.

Notes: **23** *See Louisa Jones*
Gardens of the French Riviera
*(Flammarion, 1994) and Roderick
Cameron,* The Golden Riviera
(Editions Limited, 1975).

After that, the fun began. Van Gessel loves to play with space, scale, time. He devised a central axis that goes straight from the front gate to the back. Entering from the street, you move under a long pergola, then through a passage between two houses joined at the second floor level, then into the tiny back court-yard. On each side of the pergola are regular beds, inspired both by a neighbor's vegetable plots and by the traditional layout of country curates' gardens—the village church steeple is visible from the garden. But these old-fashioned box-edged compartments have a modern look: They are com-posed of parallel lines with no perpendiculars to close them into rectangles. As often happens in contemporary design, formality here is open-ended; it does not impose order but remains play-ful, indeterminate. This is evident where exuberant plantings between the green lines are dotted with fanciful topiary—here a little tower, there a fat hen.

Michael van Gessel takes inspiration from tradition to get new ideas. One part of the house advances more than the other toward the street. In the result-ing recess is a rectangular pool, fed by a simple fountain. Its classic lines are echoed abstractly by the white framing around the windows of the build-ing, and repeated again in the whitewashed trunks of twin linden trees flanking the pergola. Generations of farmers "painted" their fruit trees in this manner to protect them from bugs and diseases. In the 1940s, at the famous Fiorentina gardens on the Riviera, Roderick Cameron adapted this treatment to citrus trees for ornamental reasons. The trick has remained in the southern design repertory ever since.[23] This garden is full of such visual echoes. It remains readable because it has few verticals— just the pergola and the twin lindens, which suffice to provide a "ceiling" for the outdoor room. The trees have been clipped into globes to allow sun-light to reach the plants underneath all year round.

At the outset, with frugal foresight, van Gessel purchased 1,100 rooted dwarf box-cuttings, which he stored in the back courtyard in a corner bed only twenty feet square. A visitor compared it to a miniature rice paddy! Two years later, the box lines of the south courtyard were planted from this stock, but many cuttings remained. It was decided to prune them in playful waves, creating a living sculpture.

A kind neighbor helped fill this garden with fruit—peaches, grapes, figs—as well as the herbs needed to make the local aperitif wine, *sautel.* "This is a garden for the limey soil and hot summers of Provence," says van Gessel, "It could not exist in Holland." The plantsmanship, however, is Dutch. The carefully orchestrated floral display is continuous, from the early *Helleborus fœtidus* to the last yellow sternbergias, known locally as harvest crocuses. From February to April, all is silver and gold, featuring the indigenous *Narcissus poeticus.* Then come dark blue aquilegia (which self-sow)

and sky-blue *Iris germanica,* overlapping with dramatic white eremurus. In summer there are lavenders and American sages, then *Anemone japonica* "Honorine Jobert," followed by Montecasino asters with their "splash of finely woven white flowers." Van Gessel's floral carpet is especially beautiful viewed from the second story balcony. It mixes native and exotic varieties, but everything must be drought-resistant.

The courtyard is no longer visible from the street, thanks to newly raised walls now topped with garlands of wisteria and roses. As one owner puts it, "We are no longer obliged to say hello to all the passersby, but we still have splendid views of the mountains just outside the village." The mountains and the inclusion of wildflower species in the beds bring the local landscape into the garden. This strong and simple design is a good example of adapting tradition graciously and imaginatively to changing customs and needs.

Above, left and right:
"The main thing," says van Gessel, "is to give each plant a chance to show off its most splendid qualities. I particularly like long-stemmed plants that disappear among other plants after flowering." White candles of eremurus emerge among the topiary and box globes.

Right:
The open plan of this parterre is a game with nature rather than order imposed.

Taking a Break

A City Office Garden

Surface: Less than 2,000 square feet.
Creator: Dominique Lafourcade (designer). Begun in 1997.

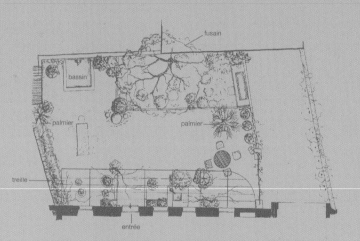

———— Bruno Lafourcade and his son Alexandre direct a company which specializes in the restoration and creation of Provençal residences in traditional styles, particularly *bastides*. Bruno's wife Dominique, born in Avignon, was first a painter before becoming one of the region's most famous garden designers.

Opposite, top,
and below right:
Contrasts of texture (foliage, paint-work, and stone) are enhanced by the play of light and shade all day long. The designer adjusts internal proportions and perspectives to blur the sense of scale and let the imagination take flight.

Below left:
The euonymus was reshaped by artist Marc Nucera.

Right:
Water gushes from an elephant's head designed by the Lafourcade's friend François Chevalier; the fountain's edges may be used as comfortable seats.

Next page:
Playful exoticism—a single, slight palm combined with a gondolier's pole.

The company's offices are located in a nineteenth-century house on the main boulevard of the fashionable town of Saint-Rémy. Bruno chose this property because of a tree—a 150-year-old euonymus growing in a courtyard sheltered by a remnant of the city's medieval stone ramparts. The building's three stories were quickly trans-formed into offices, keeping the intimate feel of the former private home. The dining room is used at times for business meetings or for gastronomic festivities—but on ordinary days, weather permitting, everyone lunches in the garden.

Dominique Lafourcade restored this tiny, L-shaped space that lies along the south side of the house, whose massive presence is soft-ened by a light trellis running the length of the façade. Such structures are traditional in the region, typical of the Mediterranean blending of year-round use and beauty. Customarily, they support a wisteria and a grapevine—both of which leaf out late, to let the sun through their elegant tracery in winter and provide shade in summer. They also offer fragrant flowers in spring, mixed foliage color and fruit in the fall. Here the trellising is only wide enough for the wisteria, but a muscat vine shades the west gate.

The door from the house opens in the middle of the façade, but bilateral symmetry is not maintained in the garden. For one thing, the magnificent euonymus is already off-center. Dominique Lafourcade's plan is formal but irregular; it uses straight lines and right angles to create surprises, not predictability. From the door, you can hear water falling into the fountain round the corner but without seeing it. A table and some chairs are comfortably close, while others are farther away, near the euonymus. Here too the disposition is double but asymmetrical, though when needed for a larger party, these informal groupings of furniture are easily reassembled. Everything is relaxed and relaxing but never banal.

The only other tree besides the euonymus is a thin palm of the sort that was fashionable in Provençal town gardens in the nineteenth century. Its exposed, hairy trunk rises from spikes of euphorbia (*Euphorbia characias* subsp. *wulfenii*) and round dark masses of Mexican orange (*Choisya ternata*). In such a shady, intimate garden, foliage counts more than flowers, and texture is important. Everything man-made has a dull, timeworn finish: rough earthenware pots, shutters and furniture with lightly peeling paint. The plants, on the contrary, have lustrous leaves that reflect light. Among them, choisyas, hebes, raphiolepis, *Chamerops humilis*, camellias, pittosporums. This rich palate of evergreens also sets off the ochre of the house

and the pale limestone of the walls. Seasonal color is provided by the wisteria and, in pots, massive oleanders with dark red flowers, which match the tablecloths and cushions. Color here is experienced for itself but also as part of the larger management of light through space. The sun moves across this courtyard from dawn to dusk, projecting ever-changing shadows on the house front as on the beige gravel surfacing. There is no lawn.

Owners of small gardens often try to make them look bigger. Dominique Lafourcade takes delight in this one's intimacy, but she carefully avoids all sense of claustrophobia by letting both the eye and the imagination travel beyond the garden's boundaries. The eastern and western walls are low enough to allow views of the neighbors and let in the sun. Each wall has a trellised gate. The western one leads to the garage, but the eastern one, just a little different from its mate, is sham. Near the palm tree, but not immediately obvious, is a green-and-white Venetian gondolier's pole.

Lafourcade enjoys blurring the visitor's sense of scale and distance, mixing fine and bold foliage, globes and sword shapes, local and exotic elements, all with a studied casualness. Thanks to these contrasts, under light which shifts from hour to hour and season to season, this tiny courtyard becomes a miniature jungle, a dream space apart where a person can enjoy losing herself for a while—before going back to work.

Family Plots

In a Var Suburb

Area: 9,700 square feet. Creators: Denis and Marie-Françoise Weis (owners).
Begun in 1993.

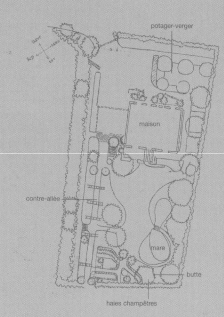

When Denis Weis first saw this site, he picked up a handful of its deep, loamy soil and decided to buy. Like his wife, a nurse, he grew up in this vineyard region and knows its resources well. Gardening has no secrets for him either: He has a degree in horticulture and has been advising the public at a highly reputed local garden center since 1986. In spite of long working days and a modest budget, he and Marie-Françoise have created a beautiful garden containing more than 200 species of plants.

Denis advises his clients to begin by taking pictures of a new garden site to help decide what needs to be screened. Then he suggests laying out the bare bones, starting from the edges, taking care to provide surprises for visitors as they walk around. Beginners should also study local wild flora and visit other gardens in the region. Denis and a colleague, Nicole Arboireau, started a garden club to help organize outings around Fréjus. The Weises also exchange plants with their friends, Pierre and Monique Cuche, whose books on Mediterranean gardening have helped many gardeners get started in Provence.[24]

For their own home, the Weises imagined an original layout with an outside path circling a central space of rough grass, visible from all angles. Denis feels that the resulting cross-perspectives "make the whole thing seem much bigger than it is. When you are in the center, you look up toward the sky." Another idea is the juxtaposition of two paths next to each other but separated along the west side. Visitors begin by taking the path against the outer hedge and exit along the other (parallel to the first, but separated from it by pergolas draped with old-fashioned rambling roses).

Once inside, there is much to discover, even in such a small space: a tiny orchard and vegetable plot, a box garden ("verging on the Japanese"), and a pond with a small bridge backed by a ridge framing faraway views of the

Above:
The open heart of the garden is the children's play field. All around are secret corners with rare plants, including the long pergola of the double path.

Following pages, Left:
The gate leading into the Japanese-inspired box-garden between two Duprez cypresses.

Right:
Orchard and vegetable garden combined.

Notes: [24] *Pierre Cuche,* Jardins du Midi *(Édisud, 1997);* Plantes du Midi, *volumes 1 and 2 (Édisud, 1998);* La Palette des saisons au Jardin *(Édisud, 2002).*

hills beyond. Half smothered by the plants, the house does not dominate the garden. Shuttered windows peak through the foliage.

Denis takes care to harmonize groupings rather than show off individual treasures. His model is the English mixed border with pictures following one after the other throughout the season. There are big differences, however. He forgoes the profuse summer flowering and green lawns of England, neither of which is adapted to this climate. And while he collects every category of plant from bulbs to tall conifers, his particular favorites are spring- and fall-flowering shrubs and roses. In summer, he adds color with pots brought out for the purpose, but in actual fact he prefers foliage to flowers. He cherishes his bamboos, rejecting the idea that they are not for small gardens. After all, he reminds us, most Japanese gardens are in small spaces also. Despite the fact that conifers have been out of fashion for some years now, Denis has grouped a selection by size and color on the ridge, next to tall deciduous trees that turn to flame in the fall.

His great pride is his mixed country-style hedges. Along the boundary of the lot are planted no fewer that thirty big trees, rising above a strip of mixed shrubs. From outside the garden, strollers from the housing development next door can enjoy a magic display of photinias, eleagnus, and rambling roses. Denis likes to mix one third evergreen species with

Opposite:
Beyond the pond is a view
of the Var countryside.

Above:
Denis tucks objects and
sculpture that he makes
himself into every corner.

two thirds deciduous in his hedges. During the great heat wave of 2003, he lost only a few varieties, while hedges made up of a single species died completely. Upkeep is minimal: he prunes only to limit expansion. Compost makes itself when leaves fall; he just adds a little manure. There is no digging because of the bulbs. If a tree outgrows its space, it can be stooled—cut back close to the ground. Its neighbors will hide and protect it until it gets back into shape. Another big advantage of this freeform hedging is that it attracts wildlife. For Denis and Marie-Françoise, even the smallest of gardens can serve as a wildlife shelter if its walls and hedges are put to good use. This garden is certainly well-populated, first by its creators, who spend an average of two hours a day working in it, then by all the sculpted animals which Denis makes himself from a variety of materials, and finally by the Weis children who play hide and seek here with their friends. Clearly everything prospers here.

Sculpture in Camera

A Restaurant Garden in Monaco

Area: 1,600 square feet. Creator: Alain Faragou (landscape architect).
Begun in 2003 (finished in six months).

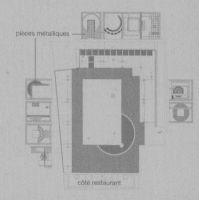

pièces métalliques

côté restaurant

Alain Faragou calls himself a "Mediterranean digest."[25] Born in North Africa of southern French and Italian parents, he grew up on the French Riviera. After studying both horticulture and garden design, he became a landscape architect with a degree from the Parisian École supérieure d'architecture des jardins et du paysage.

Notes: [25] *See Faragou's website in address list on p.266, and his book* Le Parc Fernand Braudel, La Seyne-sur-Mer *(Édisud, 2001).*

Since 1978 he and his wife, Geneviève, have been running a design agency, which handles everything from royal parks in the Middle East to urban projects in France, including city approaches, newly developed industrial zones, housing developments, stadiums and parks, highway plantings, and a whole new section of the city of Grasse. Faragou has traveled to visit gardens worldwide and several times met the Brazilian garden designer Roberto Burle Marx with whom he shares two goals: "the practice of landscape design as a contemporary art, and the protection of native species."

Faragou considers that gardens and landscapes are of the same essence. His website states quite simply, "Private landscape gardening, urban design, and management of the larger landscape: all three depend on a complex and subtle association among similar elements." Of

course he recognizes that different categories exist and is interested in all. In those neighborhoods of modern cities where social unrest is strongest, where streets are overflowing with bars, parking lots, and cheap housing, Faragou fights to find room for a garden, however small. Size and scale make no difference to his approach and certainly would not suffice to distinguish landscape from garden. Whether it is in vast projects like the municipal parks at La Seyne-sur-Mer and Martigues, or in a tiny courtyard in Monaco, he begins in the same way. He explores the potential of the site, gains an understanding of both its cultural and natural history, and then proposes a complete design.

The restaurant of the prestigious Automobile Club in Monaco has an outdoor terrace, a simple rectangle that extends out from the dining room. It already contained a palm and two citrus trees, mixed plantings, and a lot of concrete. Faragou

Above and right:
The center space of the restaurant terrace has to remain open for the display of trophies like those of the Grand Prix de Monaco. Among the many varieties planted between the metal cutouts are tall, freeform plants like brugmansia, freylinia, lagerstroemia, callistemon, maple, erythrina, and dombeya. Pruned into shapes are dwarf and variegated pittosporums, pieris, *Camellia sassanqua*, melianthus, thevetia, sparrmannia, grevillea, and westringia. Climbers include solanums, Chinese wisteria, white flowering plumbagos, *Clematis armandii*, blue and pink hardenbergias, honeysuckles, pink *Podranea ricasoliana*, and jasmines. To ensure continuous flowering there are peonies, orange-red abutilons, agapanthus, *Hedychiums coronarium* and *flavescens*, clivia, thunbergia, and various old roses.

was asked to imagine a space that would be beautiful, appeal to customers, and provide the setting for exhibits and events like the celebration of the Grand Prix. In the far corners, two service entrances giving directly onto the street behind needed to be carefully hidden.

To deal with all these requirements, Faragou created a clever structure that combines architecture, sculpture, and a living garden. He lined the three walls with overlapping panels of metal cut-outs that use shapes evoking automobile parts—here a suspension cable, there a gearbox. These vertical elements are superimposed four deep, but staggered to set off their silhouettes and to leave room between them for plants. The metal used is Cor-ten steel, which rusts slightly without deteriorating. Each panel was meticulously designed to obtain an exact balance of depth and sequence. The result is a kind of continuous living sculpture with developing themes, its effects changing throughout the day as the sun moves overhead. In the evening, it can be lit by four possible built-in lighting schemes, programmed to simulate dawn or sunset, provide backlighting, or dramatize the plantings.

Plants in impressive variety were chosen for their graphic shapes, but also to provide an avalanche of color all through the season. Before planting, the soil was changed to a depth of roughly two feet. Faragou wanted to create an impression of "slightly wild-looking exuberance," but regular pruning is necessary to keep the right balance between the frames and the plants. The crowns of existing trees suffice to create shade and give an impression of a ceiling for this outdoor room. For the middle of the garden, Faragou chose *Dichondra repens* rather than

lawn. Outlined with a strip of green, white and black marble, the symmetry of the rectangle is broken at the corner near the entrance, where a circle replaces the right angle. Faragou and his team are particularly careful about the patterning and materials used for surfacing.

The designer considers this garden to be "a living allegory of automobile travel." He particularly likes the "architectural blending of tree trunks and foliage with the metallic lines and curves." Intercrossing sight lines and volumes have been carefully balanced. The result is an original conception with a meticulous construction, an adventure that goes far beyond mere restaurant décor.

Land Art, Japanese Style

A Farm with a View in the Luberon

Area: Lower courtyard about 2,200 square feet; upper level 3,000 square feet.
Creators: Nicole de Vésian (designer), Alain-David Idoux (designer), Jean-Claude
Rim (garden restorer), and Marc Nucera (Land Artist). Begun in 1994.

A British-American couple scouting for a vacation home met Alain-David Idoux, who, by then in his thirties, had become a "sculptor of landscapes." Raised in Provence, later professor at Beaux-Arts schools in Israel, Paris, and Caen, Idoux was a pioneer in the new Provençal Land Art.[26]

Notes: [26] *There are unfortunately few accounts of the work of Alain-David Idoux. See Louisa Jones,* Le Nouvel Esprit des Jardins: un art, un savoir-faire en Provence *(Hachette, 1998) and Paige Dickey,* Breaking Ground *(Stewart, Tabori & Chang, 2004).*

Left:
The "jewel box" or enclosed
courtyard, which uses very simple
but asymmetrical elements with
great harmony.

Opposite, left:
The steps linking the two levels,
shaded by a leaning tree trunk
(Robinia pseudoacacia).

Right:
The upper level with its pool, looking toward the cloud plantings.

Following pages:
The sculpted landscape, seen
from inside and out.

He worked for some time with Nicole de Vésian, a fashion stylist who retired to Provence from Paris where she had founded the New Vision studio, located in a restored coal cellar right next to the Elysée Palace (residence of the French presidents). Asked to design shoes, cars, and yachts, Vésian also invented the famous pleated scarf for Hermès. In the south, she created a garden of stone and clipped green-ery, now considered to be one the world's leading models for dry climate gardening, both elegant and wild (pp. 13, 135). Toward the end of her life, she

was visited by famous Japanese garden designers with whom she had marked affinities. Idoux and Vésian both died in the late 1990s—he tragically young, she soon after her eightieth birthday.

It was Idoux who persuaded the couple to buy the Fontaine des Faucons, an eighteenth-century farmstead on the edge of a hilltown, surrounded by orchards and vineyards, with a panoramic view to the west. Nicole de Vésian restored the house and began working on the gardens, before being stopped by a minor car accident. Idoux then took over and finished the upper terrace and the

plantings. Later on, Jean-Claude Rim, a specialist in garden restoration, pulled the somewhat neglected pieces together again. Rim also engaged Marc Nucera, a plant sculptor trained by both Idoux and Vésian, to help give the garden new life.

There are in fact two gardens at the Fontaine des Faucons: the lower courtyard, entirely enclosed, and the upper plateau, which opens onto the greater landscape. The owners wondered in the beginning how they would ever manage to connect these two levels. Vésian designed a beautifully simple stone staircase as the main link. It is shaded by the twisted trunk and crown of an old robinia and flanked by green globes, a marriage of greenery and stonework typical of both of the original designers. The almost minimal symmetry of the building is set off by evergreen and evergray plantings, which are carefully shaped and grouped but always resolutely asymmetrical. Their forms and volumes harmonize, but no shape is ever

repeated exactly. Each plant remains individual.

Above, a swimming pool lies under the crest of the hill, invisible from below. From its balustrade, looking down to the house courtyard, you discover a whole series of nicely chosen and well-placed details—a pot, a trellis, one or two chairs—creating gentle rhythms in soft tones. This courtyard is certainly an outdoor room, but its aspect and mood depend on the choice of vantage point.

The main masterpiece of this garden lies beyond the west end of the pool, where a path leads off to the valley. From the pool, all you can make out are the feathery heads of tamarisks around a tall juniper, which seems to float on the horizon. You are drawn to this spot, sensing something more. As the owner says, "In Alain's gardens, you always want to go farther and see what lies beyond!" Here you need only go about twenty yards to discover a giant living sculpture crisscrossed with paths, composed mainly of shrubs pruned into Japanese

cloud shapes, breathtakingly beautiful. The plants chosen are mainly local wild species: laurustinus, junipers, rosemary, bay laurel, Aleppo pines. But others seem more exotic: yuccas, dwarf fan palms (in fact indigenous to the region), and hypericum. Paths paved with stone slabs offer several choices, making this a mini maze. The topsoil is thin, and rough rock emerges here and there. The whole valley unfolds beyond this steep slope, revealing the medieval hilltown close by, a vast field of lavender farther down, then blue hills like waves. Idoux loved blurring the outer edges of his gardens. The enclosed courtyard remained for him a kind of jewel box, but this sculpted transition, the first of a series of planes leading to panoramic landscape, was in fact a "boundary" opening onto infinity.

The view is best appreciated from an intimate aperitif corner nearby, a favorite spot for the owners and their guests. All around the house are simple, elegant but also welcoming plantings that need little upkeep. Never is there a gardenesque feel but always a sense of wild nature, transformed into living art before melting into the surrounding landscape.

Story telling

Every garden tells at least one story: how it came to be. Some are also divided into separate chapters, to be experienced one after the other. The landscape movement of the late eighteenth century organized whole countrysides into a series of pictures to be enjoyed as an elegant promenade, and if a village did not fit the composition, it and all its inhabitants were packed up and moved to the right location![27] A narrative garden can relate either its own story or one imported from elsewhere. Stourhead, a leading eighteenth-century example in England, depicts events from Virgil's epic poem, the *Aeneid*. Today in Provence, nurseryman Jean-Marie Rey illustrates the voyages of Odysseus with olive stumps set among rambling rosemaries, in an area of only 500 square feet. The Alchemist's Gardens (p. 158) offer a quest for spiritual initiation through connected garden rooms. Here, as at Stourhead, explanations are provided in the form of inscriptions to guide the traveler en route. The owner of one new garden in Provence plans to lay out the story of his life in compartments, with the help of a famous designer and contemporary sculptors (p.166).

Narrative gardens with several chapters have usually been big. The first examples in southern France were ambitious Riviera estates made in the early twentieth century, like the Villa Île de France on Cap Ferrat. There Béatrice de Rothschild designed elaborate compositions evoking a series of far-off countries, imagining her peninsula as a vast ocean liner and dressing her gardeners as sailors.[28] In England at that time, at Hidcote Manor, Lawrence Johnston was creating a more intimate version of the serial garden with "green rooms," each different, closed off from its neighbors by hedging. In those days, it was customary to remodel the site completely and start with a clean slate. Today's multiple gardens tend to incorporate existing features—even dead trees may be

winding path on a wild hillside, the itinerary shifts from one section to the next. The house in this case is merely a point of departure and may soon disappear from view. In the second case, the house remains central, like the hub of a wheel. Each of its aspects presents a different mood and may also have a different function. Visitors may move in sequence round the circle, but the owners are more likely to choose one direction or another according to whether they wish to play tennis, dig up carrots, or go swimming. Of course the two models may mix, as in many of the great Italian gardens or at Serre de la Madone, the Riviera winter garden of Lawrence Johnston, the same man who created the "green rooms" at Hidcote. In his French design, one part of the visitor's circuit involves moving round the house, always visible, but another leads off into mysterious byways up and down the terraced hillside. [31]

The "domino" style lends itself well to the linear organization of formal gardens, like those made for Pierre Bergé by Michel Semini (p. 52), or the private gardens of decorators Jean-Louis Raynaud and Kenyon Kramer. In a recently created example, English designer Tim Rees mixed parterres and meadows in a vast composition where the unveiling of various parts covers many acres. The visit moves around the house, but the circle is so far-flung that it seems linear. Rees was inspired to replace certain hedges by gentle slopes planted with a free mix of perennials and Mediterranean subshrubs, creating dynamic connection as much as

treated as sculptures. People want to acknowledge and incorporate site memory. The German poet Goethe once wrote that "gardens are places which weave together the threads of the ephemeral and the everlasting. Yet nothing is so momentary that it does not leave some trace, some image of its passing."[29] Landscape architects today often compare land to a palimpsest, a tablet on which one scribe writes over the last without ever completely removing the traces of former versions.

The first great contemporary gardens in western Provence all tell stories with many chapters: the Jas Créma in the Mont Ventoux region, the Petit Fontanille in the Alpilles, and Les Confines, the garden of Dominique Lafourcade near Avignon.[30] In the last two, devoted owners still add new parts almost every year.

There are at least two ways of laying out serial gardens on a grand scale. In the first case, the sequence is linear, as in a game of dominos. Whether it leads through formal green rooms enclosed by hedging or along a

separation between the parts. Hedges are reserved for wind protection and to outline the most formal parts, such as the topiary garden, but they never block the intriguing view of nearby hills.

Home gardeners rarely determine their entire layout all at once, some chapters being written before others in a more haphazard manner. This more experimental situation can also be richly inventive. Incident is determined by various factors, by the lay of the land or by some change in its use. At the Vallon Raget, a Provençal family shared a property rented to a tenant farmer for over thirty years. As he grew old and stopped working certain sections, the owners reclaimed them to make gardens. In the Luberon, Ione Tézé began her garden in the style of her friend Nicole de Vésian (p. 40), enlarged it through the years, and has most recently been influenced by Gilles Clément. Near Apt, La Chabaude was first restored by Alain-David Idoux with the help of Nicole de Vésian, with the goal of creating different landscapes for each aspect. Today's owners

are working on an itinerary that will link all the varied episodes of this complex tale.

Whether the story told is linear or circular in its layout, or a mix of the two, transitions count as much as the content of each chapter. The site itself often makes the decisions. Flat space offers limitless possibilities; it is the empty page of the poets that requires a powerful vision to fill. Hilly land, much more common in Provence, already suggests moods and episodes. Wooded slopes lend themselves to landscape gardening, while terraced hillsides are already a kind of Land Art.

[27] *For a detailed history of the great movement, see the books already cited of John Dixon Hunt as well as* The Picturesque Garden in Europe *(Thames and Hudson, 2003) and* Greater Perfections: The Practice of Garden Theory *(Thames and Hudson, 2000).* [28] *See Louisa Jones,* Gardens of the French Riviera *(Flammarion, 1994).* [29] *Goethe,* Les affinités électives; *trans. Jean-Pierre du Colombier (Gallimard, 1954), p. 254.* [30] *See Gardens in Provence, op. cit.* [31] *See Louisa Jones,* Serre de la Madone *(Actes Sud, 2001). Available in English from the author.*

Left page, above left:
An elegant garden at the Mas du Grès, created by Jean-Louis Raynaud and Kenyon Kramer.

Above right:
Attractive detailing in the garden of Ione Tézé.

Below:
The woodland pool of the Vallon Raget.

Above left:
The landscape garden of La Chabaude.

Right:
A parterre of olive trees, silver santolinas, and germander by Tim Rees in a multipart garden in the Alpilles.

Virtuoso Variations

The Domino Courtyards of Pierre Bergé

Area: Roughly half an acre; each of the two new courtyards is about 6,500 square feet.
Creators: Michel Semini (designer), Hugues Bosc (architect), Pierre Bergé (owner).
Main garden begun in 1993; two new courtyards begun 2001-2002.

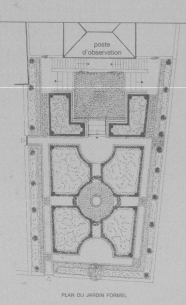

PLAN DU JARDIN FORMEL

Fashion mogul Pierre Bergé wanted a vacation home in Provence that would be more intimate than the celebrated gardens he shares with Yves Saint-Laurent in Deauville and Marrakech. Starting with a modest house on the edge of the town of Saint-Rémy-de-Provence, he gradually bought up neighboring properties. The result is a series of courtyards linked like dominoes, separated from the street and other houses by high walls on three sides.

The west opens onto olive orchards underplanted with meadow flowers. This countryside area is still really part of the garden, since the entire property (eighteen acres in all), is completely fenced in. The central courtyard is entered by passing first through a very discreet small door, then a small forecourt near the kitchen, then another small door—no grand entrance here! The main section of the garden is shaded by broad-crowned trees, with each trunk set in a raised circle of aromatic plants. Next door is the swimming pool, with its twin parterres of "Iceberg" roses and a floral carpet looking toward the greenhouse. Beyond this is a Moroccan patio with guest houses, a bougainvillea-decked pergola, and a ceramic fountain. In the other direction, an enclosure centered on an octagonal fountain precedes two sections added since 2000: a cottage garden and a formal parterre.

Designer Michel Semini grew up in Nice, then began his garden career in Paris after training with botanist Edouard d'Avdeew in 1971. Once established, he returned to the south to become one of Provence's most successful designers. Since 1973, Semini has collaborated regularly with architect Hugues Bosc. In the Bergé garden, each courtyard is an "outdoor room" where harmony with the house is crucial. Collaboration between these two professionals and the owner can be felt strongly in the results.

Semini's style is already architectural. He controls space by juxtaposing stone and sculpted greenery to create subtle geometries which are never hard or rigid—or predictable. Each compartment has its own scale and colors, and appeals to the eye on different levels. In each can be found a different harmony between intimacy

From left to right:
The swimming pool tapestry
seen from the greenhouse mixes
globes of silver germander
(*Teucrium fruticans*) with
Ceratostigma plumbago, whose
foliage turns red in the fall; the
small Moroccan garden; the
octagonal fountain; the main
courtyard; the pool of the
cottage garden.

Notes: [32] *See Marie Mauron,*
Le Printemps de la Saint-Martin
(Atelier Marcel Jullian, 1979).

and open perspectives, determined in part by
the need to screen unwanted structures outside.
Semini, not a horticulturalist, has chosen resis-
tant plant varieties that have done well in this
region for a long time. There is no lawn here;
instead, careful attention is paid to paving textures, materials, and small differences of level.

The designer's basic evergreen structure
allows for seasonal variation of a particularly
theatrical kind, such as the dramatic moment in
May when pots of red flowering hibiscus are
brought out of the greenhouse to be set all over
the garden. Mystery is never sacrificed to clarity:
Most transitions are through small doors or
around unexpected turns, and some openings
actually turn out to be mirrors! The trickle

of water leads you onward, since water is
present, variously staged, in each garden.

From the beginning, Pierre Bergé counted
on the purchase of one neighboring house in
particular. It once belonged to folk writer Marie
Mauron, who described her "wild" garden[32] as
a place where Roman ruins mix with humble
country flowers as well as more exotic species.
An oleander variety was once created in her
honor by the famous Rey nurseries, blending a
native variety with another from Afghanistan.
Today when gardeners are much aware of site
memory, few plots can claim as rich a heritage as
this one. Around Marie Mauron's long pergola,
Semini designed a Provençal cottage garden
overflowing with color, fragrance, flowers, and fruit.

Left:
Doors and windows are everywhere mysterious.

Opposite:
The well of the cottage garden with Marie Mauron's pergola.

Following pages:
The formal garden glimpsed though its small door and from the upper level.

Beyond this luxuriant scene is the second recent addition: a formal parterre, almost austere, planted with cypress and olive trees. Pyramids, globes, straight lines and curves are all carved out of box, bay, and *Viburnum tinus*, while inside the patterning grows a wide range of aromatic plants. Almond trees provide verticals in the heart of the garden, and a tall silver-leafed linden closes the main sightline. The whole composition can be looked at from an "observation deck" one story above (made from a former house). It allows you a rare view outside the garden, onto olive orchards and the town beyond. Will the domino series stop here? For some designers, such a series is a mere vehicle for design virtuosity. But for Semini and Bosc—as for their client, so distinguished a figure in the fashion world—style is never superficial. The refinement displayed in these gardens reveals a complete mastery of many arts.

Old-fashioned Country Living

A Bastide in the Alpilles

Area: About 3.5 acres. Creators: Dominique Lafourcade (designer),
Bruno and Alexandre Lafourcade (interior designers). Begun in 2001.

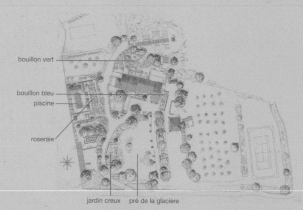

bouillon vert

bouillon bleu

piscine

roseraie

jardin creux   pré de la glacière

_____ The word *bastide* appears everywhere in
Provence today, not always appropriately.[33] It has come to
conjure up a Provençal "globes and pots" style that has
inspired gardens from California to Australia. Although often
spoiled in France by industrial pastiche, this model in fact
adapts very well to contemporary needs.

Notes : [33] *Nerte Fustier Dautier,* Les Bastides de Provence et leurs Jardins *(Serg, 1977) and Gilles Mihière,* La Provence au temps des bastides *(Aubanel, 2004).*

n expert hands, its best examples still attain the vernacular ideal described by historian Victor Papanek, where "structures, made of local materials, economically apt, fit in well with local climate, flora, fauna, ways of life. Never self-conscious, they recede into the environment rather than serving as self-proclaiming design statements. Human in scale, they have a sensual frugality that results in true elegance."[34]

The Lafourcade family has been happily cultivating this approach for decades (see p. 20). Dominique is famous for her gardens. Bruno and his son Alexandre restore period houses and make new ones in traditional styles. As a family, they possess a long experience of local craft know-how. Every new project begins with a close, on-site study. "In the old days," says Bruno, "people sat on a stone and asked themselves, What is the prevailing wind? That is what building is all about, it is not just surveys and contour lines."[35]

The Lafourcades' clients for this project were a couple wanting a retirement home where comfort and ease blended with elegance and charm. Both gave up northern family châteaux to choose instead this golden *bastide*, shaded by old trees of impressive stature: hackberries (*Celtis australis*), a linden, cypress, and pines. Once farmed, this estate is entirely surrounded by walls. Vestiges of former constructions add a lot of character: an ice-house built into the entry wall, a spring head, and above all a long stone canal, raised like a wall, which cuts diagonally through the park. These ruins have now been integrated into the subtle play on levels that anchors the house to its site. From the entrance gate, the gardens descend pleasantly graded planes where hedges, trees, and fountains outline squares and rectangles until you

(see p. 20)

Above left:
Steps lead down to the pool with its columns.

Above right and opposite:
The house sits in the heart of the garden like the hub of a wheel. The access road reveals slight differences of level, arranged in plateaux. The eye is immediately drawn towards the striking twin roofs beside the pool, their form echoed by the square parasol shading the house terrace.

Following pages left:
An old cistern overlooks the rose garden above the pool.

Right:
Majestic trees add great character here, as do ruins like this old ice-house set into the garden wall.

arrive at the swimming pool, hidden from view because it occupies the lowest level.

Dominique Lafourcade calls this a "belvedere house," because on all sides you can look down on different gardens. Each area has been designed to be seen from above as well as within and without. The meadow opposite the ice-house remains relatively open to set off the main façade, but everything else is organized in sequence: the "hollow garden" overflows in spring with yellow bloom; the *boules* terrace has a little box maze wandering among its lindens. There is an herb garden and a more formal courtyard by the house, near a gnarled olive tree, for outdoor dining. Squares of roses and peonies help hide the swimming pool from

view. Behind the house is a small potager. All of this can be glimpsed from the wide paths that beckon enticingly from under the trees, as from the many windows and balconies of the house.

With her usual creativity, Lafourcade invented for this site a new type of garden that she calls "bubbles" because, seen from above, the plantings look "like a pot of simmering broth." The blue bubbles appear as a tiny terrace on the east side, planted with lavenders, perovskia, and so on, set right under the caretakers' windows. The green bubbles behind the house were planted around low stone walls and rough outcrops of rock, to create a semi-wild slope. Waves of plants have been pruned into soft cushions: abelias, escallonias, cotoneasters. These are unusual choices in Provence but lend themselves to this design and remain beautiful all year round, though their flowers and berries mark the changing seasons.

Soon there will also be a little orchard down the hill. Farther down is the secret wood, a tennis court, and a children's playhouse, which gives onto a new almond orchard near the garage. All the transitions remain flowing, natural-looking, and admirably discreet. Visitors often say of this park: "It looks as if it had always been here." In fact, only the trees and the ruins are old. But this response is a homage to the success of a *bastide* conversion that successfully adapts tradition to contemporary vision.

Notes: [34] *Quotation from the excellent book by Victor Papenek,* The Green Imperative Econolgy and Ethics in Design and Architecture *(Thames & Hudson, 1995).* [35] *Interview notes in preparation for a private book,* Lafourcade, Restaurations, constructions, créations *(2003).*

Natural Exoticism by the Sea

A Golden Villa in the Var

Area: 1.2 acres. Creators: Jean-Laurent Félizia and his company
Mouvements et paysages (designers). Begun in 1999.

——————— An abandoned park on the Var coast is now a
luxuriant garden where a family with young children lives
much of the year. Their villa was built in 1936 for the
Countess de Lesseps, whose famous uncle built the Suez
Canal. Its golden volumes, simple and strong, are set off
by striking rock formations and by the opulence and variety
of carefully orchestrated plantings.

Jean-Laurent Félizia, the garden designer, was for many years head gardener at the Domaine du Rayol, a nearby park created by French ecologist Gilles Clément to display biomes from Mediterranean climates worldwide. Félizia learned much from Clément but now has his own agency, Mouvements et paysages (Movement and landscapes). His ideal is to make "thoughtful gardens that obey the logic both of nature and of the client." He considers himself to be "an ally of nature who animates and accompanies, whether in hard landscaping, pruning, or planting." His team of nine both creates and maintains gardens, thus solving a major problem for most designers: the afterlife of their work. Félizia belongs to a new generation of "gardenists" who refuse to separate conceptualizing, poetry, technology, and botany from hands-on manual labor.

Restoration of this site meant recycling as much stonework as possible from earlier days and preserving fine old cork oaks and Aleppo pines (now grown into picturesque shapes). There is now a walk round the garden, beginning at the gate below in the southwest corner, circling east around the house to the pool, moving along the north edge, and coming back down to the entrance on a broad stone staircase. Its generous proportions are another vestige of 1930s design. Félizia emphasizes major arteries by outlining them dramatically with bright bloom. But there are also many hidden footpaths up and down the hill, where the children love to play hide-and-seek. There is no lawn, but a few areas are carpeted with zoysia (always so pleasantly elastic to walk on).

The property is densely planted, boasting over 200 species. Many are native or long-term

Above left and opposite:
Small pockets of soil beside steps and paths lend themselves to exuberant but drought-resistant plantings: polygonums, euphorbias, oreganos, tiny aloes, *petasites,* and even at times palms.

Above right:
The Treasure Island atmosphere is reinforced by a doll's house hidden in the wood.

Following pages:
Stone is always present here but never mere décor, even the paving is a form of sculpture.

PAGES 72-73:
Near the 1930s staircase, *Verbena bonariensis* and an Argentinean solanum sow themselves happily among the pines and cork oaks.

residents: cistus, perennial geraniums, wall-flowers (*Matthiola canescens*, commonly found here by the sea), and the great Portuguese shrub heathers. Dwarf fan palms, also indigenous to these parts, look exotic mixed with yuccas, agaves, aloes, and date palms. Félizia's judicious eye keeps this mini jungle balanced, setting off swordlike shapes with globes and cascading plants. He establishes an appropriate scale for each section, from the smallest aloes edging steps to the giant palm rockery screening the pool. Rough rock and stone structures are always there to impose rigor: a section of wall, a staircase, a pebble mosaic where two paths meet. Proportions and perspectives are also maintained by the masterful but gentle pruning of certain trees, which the owner regards as beautiful sculptures.

Everywhere sounds, fragrance, and color echo back and forth, beginning with the sea below, cooing like a dove or roaring like a lion, according to its mood. The honey scent of a *myriophyllus* rises with the perfume of orange blossoms from a sheltered corner near the pool. For the owner, this garden is a paradise magically imported from somewhere distant and exotic, like South America. "What I really love here," she adds, "is the fact that this luxuriance persists even in severe drought! Here, you know, we begin to cut back on watering in March so our plants will be ready for the summer heat."

For Félizia, a good gardenist must know his site intimately, as well as the plants he uses, in order to manage both in harmony. When working with Gilles Clément, he learned to immerse

himself in the ecosystems evolving in each locality. He regards his creations as an endless series of experiments, a never-finished process. This approach can be disconcerting for some clients! Those who accept it, like the owners of this garden, get some wonderful surprises in exchange—such as the giant candelabra euphorbia that Félizia saved from an old garden about to be bulldozed. He brought it here as a gift, though four men were necessary to carry it. Creativity for Félizia means a marriage of imagination and vigilance: "You can slip so quickly from a garden with meaning to one that has none," he says, adding, "This garden is very showy, but also very mysterious."

Cliff Hanging

An Eagle's Nest in the Luberon

Area: The upper terrace and the lower garden together: about 1 acre.
Creators: the owners, Michel Biehn (designer), Jean-Claude Appy (nurseryman),
and others. Begun in 1997.

This exceptional site on the edge of a medieval hilltown embraces two levels separated by a two-hundred-foot retaining wall. Above is a series of courtyards, and below, grassy slopes. The upper terracing, in five small interlocking sections, commands a panoramic view of the entire valley. The nearby house already tells many stories. Begun as an eleventh-century fortification, it later served as barracks, a convent, a hospice, and finally an aristocratic residence, before being almost totally abandoned.

The garden's lower level has rows of mature cherry trees and crumbled stone walls that bear witness to an earlier layout. In 1993, a violent storm undermined the high wall, and in one night half the upper terrace hurtled downward. One huge boulder has remained, like a meteor split in two, deeply embedded in the grass. It provides a most unusual link between the two parts.

An American couple began working on this property in 1997, courageously facing this disaster as well as the general state of ruin and extremely difficult access. The fallen wall was rebuilt, using advanced technology behind a traditional appearance. A giant crane lifted materials and mature trees from the road below, and the "flying cypresses" of this garden amazed people in the region for years. When basic repair work was finished, however, the question remained: How to make sense of the two levels in a way that would be both beautiful and practical on a day-to-day basis?

The owners first engaged Nicole de Vésian (pp. 13, 40, 135), with whom they shared a

common love of gardens with lots of rough stone. Vésian hoped to find a hidden staircase in the cliff that would provide an internal connection. When she passed away, the owners called in English designer John Brookes, a specialist in "outdoor rooms." Brookes laid out the basic structure and designed a parterre for the house terrace that involved some eighty-four different varieties of perennials. Its contemporary outline was meant to echo the patchwork patterns of distant fields. "It was too modern for us," say the owners, for whom horticulture as such has few attractions. However, this consultation and another with British designer Tim Rees helped them define their own preferences. Finally, for the upper level, they decided on a simple series of rectangles where dwarf box surrounds herbs and plants with white flowers. Michel Biehn, who was already working on the interiors (p. 124), extended his talents to the garden. They also engaged nurseryman Jean-Claude Appy to help create, says Biehn, "a garden which is perfectly adjusted to the landscape as well as in harmony with a house exceptional in both its architecture and in its history."[36] Appy provided reliable local plants and a talented mason, Max Ellena, who built elegant steps and walls. The owners, in boots and jeans, participated in every stage of the work. Biehn still recalls, "This immense project unfolded like a game, like a conversation, brilliant and light but never facile."

Above:
Vegetable gardens and orchards on the lower level are a place for happy, relaxed activity.

Following pages:
The footpath links upper and lower levels, while the boulder, split in two, is now a giant garden sculpture.

Notes: **36** *This domain was photo-graphed by Gilles Martin-Raget for a recent book:* Michel Biehn's Healthy Recipes: International Cuisine from a Provençal Table *(Flammarion, 2003). The quotations from Biehn were taken from this book or from interview notes by Louisa Jones.*

It was Biehn who came up with the idea of a basket on an antique winch to allow picnics to be lowered to the swimming pool below. "It is great fun," he explains. "You lean over the wall and send down a bottle of wine—it is a very personal connection in human terms." This improvised elevator does not work for people, however, who still have to walk down by circling around the village church and passing under an ancient portal. A tiny door, like something out of *Alice's Adventures in Wonderland,* then admits them to the lower garden. This unfolds like a magical bit of countryside, its rustic promenade in pleasant contrast to the more formal terraces above. It is also a place for active living, with its swimming pool, children's playground, three little vegetable gardens, and restored orchard. A zigzagging path leads up to a gazebo with a dance floor, used in summer for family parties and sometimes elaborate *fêtes champêtres*. Nor is the fallen boulder forgotten: "It stays right in the heart of the garden," says the owner. "No one can say we don't accommodate nature!"

Nature is right at home here, but imaginatively transformed. A woman's eye sets the tone, sensitive to slight differences in level, in volume, in texture, in the quality of light. She also appreciates soft colors, a certain austerity, a subtle balance between careful detailing and harmonious overviews. This site, which offers so much variety, has provided her with constantly renewed opportunities to bring into play her personal vision, her hands, and her heart.

A Giant Riviera Rockery

A Seafront Villa Near Cannes

Area: About 2 acres on a steep hill. Creators: Jean Mus (designer),
Jean-Michel Wilmotte (architect). Begun in 2000.

_____ Riviera designer Jean Mus worships the olive
tree, as it has grown for centuries on terraced hillsides near
Grasse, near where Mus grew up: "My gardens are conceived
in its honor, to set off its beauty without disturbing its growth."[37]
Today, Mus practices his Mediterranean *savoir faire* from
California to Greece. He notes a growing fashion for palm
trees, a new taste for exoticism.

Notes: [37] *Quotations from Jean Mus, Les Jardins de Provence (Le Chêne, 1996), and interview notes from his guided visit of this garden.*

At the same time, Provençal *bastides* and manor houses are being restored in a contemporary mode sometimes called "minimalist." Mus watches these changes with equanimity: "We need a new style in Provence for this young century, something more than lavender and box globes and pots of rosemary. We need to find a coherent approach adapted to our new ways of living."

For this project on the Esterel coast, Mus decided to "invite palm trees" to join his cherished olives. He created theatrical effects that hark back to the grand gala days of the French Riviera, when the Blue Train used to bring travelers from Paris to Nice. Two-toned agaves emerging from rust-colored boulders remind Mus of the 1930s railroad posters advertising that famous journey. Brilliant hues enhance the

palms in this garden. Both the designer and the French architect Jean-Michel Wilmotte conducted here "a new experiment in color coordination," taking inspiration from the deep orange-red local granite to adjust the tones of the house, the garden, and terra-cotta pots ordered especially in Italy.

Jean Mus is known for his love of symmetry, but in this instance he bursts the bounds of classic restraint to present a whole cascade of exotic scenes. Views are plunging, surprises around every corner. Balance is still imposed, however, by the coherence of the overall design that subordinates every detail to a harmonious whole. Carefully proportioned stages lead from the house to the shore, with its panorama of islands sparkling in the sun. Discreet edgings of pittosporum or myrtle line paths, to guide steps

Mus recalls with humor that French law forbids the use of boulders instead of retaining walls. But on such a slope, he explains, "I know there will be interesting outcrops just under the surface and now and then, it's like a pretty woman, you just bare one shoulder . . . and suddenly it gets interesting!" Especially when the land, as here, tumbles down toward the sea.

Following pages:
The swimming pool on two levels, with its palms, cascades, and boulders, its circular paving and especially its reflections.

in the right direction. In spite of the luxuriance and the variety of mood, nothing is superfluous. The footpaths that run across the hillside all lead somewhere, but they also let strollers meander up- and downhill without tiring, following the example of the great Russell Page, who, as Mus reminds us, "invented the right approach to Mediterranean staircases."

This property is not a compromise between classicism and exoticism, still less between tradition and modernity. Rather it illustrates the new, dynamic dialogue between architectural minimalism and exuberant plantings. The latter's vocabulary belongs to the new wild gardening styles: cascades instead of fountains or fountains disguised as cascades; outcroppings of rough rock rather than walls; an itinerary full of unpredictable episodes that offer here some

secret nook and there a panoramic sweep. "The scenes must seem to link up naturally," explains the designer, "even if the whole thing is highly contrived. Everything seems spontaneous, but in fact, nothing is at all!"

The "natural" effect of such a garden comes in part from the banishment of straight lines almost everywhere. "You might think that humans had never had a hand here!" says Mus, though everything here today (except a row of Lambert cypresses) is the result of the designer's art. To get such results, Mus even attacked the underlying rock formations—just as was done in the grand Belle Epoque gardens. Mostly, however, he has worked with the site's existing features: its geological configuration, typical of this plateau, and the wavelike formation of the hills that remind him of the Peloponnese. The

design's sight lines follow natural contours and focus on surrounding views. And although palm trees strike a spectacular exotic note around the bilevel swimming pool, which features yet another cascade, pride of place is still given to cypresses and olive trees, so deeply wedded to the place. The plant palette varies from scene to scene but draws on Mediterranean species from all over the world: different types of pittosporum, olearia, grevillea, echiums, carissas, arbutus, oleanders, terebinths, roses, westringia, lantana, myrtles, and dwarf fan palms, to cite but a few. Touch and smell are not forgotten: A little hedge of curry plants invites stroking as you pass. On summer evenings, the scent of a whole hillside of fragrant plants wafts up to the house, carried by the moist breeze from the sea. Mus explains, "Dinner outdoors becomes delightful, without anyone really knowing why." And this man from the rustic backcountry adds, with a sigh of pleasure, "This is one of the rare times I have paid hommage to the sea."

Wild and Woodland gardening

Gardeners today talk a lot about nature. "Wild" gardens proliferate, idealized versions of woodland wilderness and country meadows. Some happily maintain an existing landscape but others obtain an illusion of spontaneity through great effort and expense. The last approach is often called Romantic (especially in the United States and the Netherlands) but is closer to the eighteenth-century Picturesque. Historian Monique Mosser links the Picturesque movement to "deeply troubled times which completely changed humankind's relationship to the natural environment."[38] Times like our own.

The Picturesque had, of course, many stages and variations, some of them contradictory.

John Dixon Hunt has retraced the movement's complexities through several generations,[39] revealing a style variously known as "irregular," "landscape," or "English," although it spread to Russia, Sweden, and even the United States. In the early twentieth century, revived by influential gardenists such as Gertrude Jekyll and William Robinson, it became "a high point in garden art and artifice […] designed to evoke sentiments such as tranquility, shelter, mystery, and seclusion." Thus concludes another historian, Helen Leach, who views the Picturesque as a precursor to the "New American garden," the "self-sustaining garden," the German "nature garden," the Dutch "ecological garden" and the "marginal wild garden."[40]

All these "natural" gardens are not the same, however. French designer Gilles Clément, defending a "humanist ecology," dissociates himself completely from both the Picturesque and subsequent Romanticism. He rejects gardens that are illusions of spontaneity created with behind-the-scenes contrivances, but he also refuses the Romantic worship of untamed, sublime Nature. In the first case, we are both manipulators and spectators; in the second, humans become irrelevant or, worse, intruders. The first involves domination and the second self-abasement, but both imply distance from nature. Clément's ideal is rather a working partnership between the human species and the biosphere, active participation in the dynamics

the mind as well as the eyes and to making connections between them, rather than to providing static, pictorial scenes." [42]

The Picturesque always situates gardens in landscape, sometimes blurring boundary lines completely. This may prove perilous. The great eighteenth-century painter Sir Joshua Reynolds warned his contemporaries that garden art is essentially "a deviation from nature." He insisted that a work which eliminated "every appearance of Art or any traces of the footsteps of Man, would no longer be a garden." [43] It often happens today, in gardens where borders are hidden or erased altogether, that visitors look around and say, "But where is the garden?" Jean Mus, a Provençal designer drawn to this style (p. 84), feels that the eighteenth-century English designers were onto a good thing—if their work was appreciated, they got the credit, but if not, it was all Nature's fault!

What can a Picturesque garden be like in Provence today? Most of the eighteenth-century practitioners were from northern Europe but took inspiration from Mediterranean subjects discovered through paintings by French and Italian masters such as Claude, Poussin, and Salvatore Rosa. Provence itself had few Picturesque parks at that time. Does it make sense for southern designers to resurrect this model today, or is it another northern import like the English mixed border? There is one big difference: The Picturesque fits the southern climate and landscapes so well that spontaneous examples of the genre can be found along every country road. Travelers with the Picturesque in mind will immediately look afresh at cliffs, peaks, gorges, and grottoes, as well as trees with wind-bent and tortured trunks,

planted in clumps rather than lines (some may even be dead); tangles of indigenous greenery setting off exotic species (an invitation to imaginary voyages); rocky outcrops; heaps of pebbles and ruined walls which may be medieval, Roman or even prehistoric remnants (invitations to meditate on the fleeting moment). All these vestiges of human interaction with nature throughout the centuries are imitated in gardens today. As for worship of the sublime, Provence also has its votaries. Sculptor and garden designer Erik Borja relates the destruction of a large part of his landscape-garden in huge floods in 1993. He could not, he admits, but be fascinated by "the spectacle of unleashed nature, threatening and wild," and he found "a certain disastrous beauty" in this "incredible display of energy." [44]

Provence clearly has all the ingredients for the new Picturesque ready to hand. The authors of *Le grand livre de la France sauvage* judge,

of growth and evolution. [41] These aims belong to our time and would be incomprehensible to our ancestors. Nonetheless, John Dixon Hunt's list of ways in which the eighteenth-century Picturesque appeals to garden-makers today would not run contrary to Clément's approach. Hunt notes its "emphasis on topographical and regional specificity" and on site-adapted vegetation; its ways of "involving visitors interactively on its sites, giving wide scope for mental and imaginative stimulation," and, in the best examples, a "dedication to entertaining moreover, that the "Provence-Côte-d'Azur region with its islands, its rocky coasts, its mountains, its fragrant garrigues, its wild rivers and sunny climate is surely the most beautiful and richest in France, both for flora and fauna."[45] Thanks to government protection agencies concerned with forestry, the natural parks network, and the coastal *Conservatoire du littoral*, this heritage is protected and thriving more and more.

Gardeners all over Provence are inspired by this potential. Many now prefer water in its wilder forms: ponds rather than pools, cascades rather than fountains. Or instead of colorful floral groupings, they choose foliage tones enhanced by ever-changing patterns of light and shade, according to the time of day and the season. These are gardens to be walked in, not just looked at, and paths must meander to provide contrasts—panoramas here, secret corners there. Boundaries remain unclear: perhaps the invisible "ha-ha," or deep trench dug to prevent livestock invading the park, would keep out wild boar, the bane of all Provençal gardeners?

Wildness is not wilderness, however. People who grew up in Provence object that nature has been humanized far too long here to lend itself to Romantic northern visions. The cultural tradition works against it. The Romans, still so much a presence, idealized agriculture far more than hunting. Uncultivated land—pastures, meadows, or wooded hills—was never the opposite of farmland here but a useful complement, an alternate source of food. Christian Tamisier, a Provençal sociologist, explains that in the local language woodland is called *selve*, a term that implies proximity, domesticity, familiarity."[46] Most of the following examples remain unabashedly

agricultural. Even when death is invoked, as it so often is by the Romantics, the Provençal version substitutes gentle alliance. It is beautifully expressed by Marie Mauron, a local author of peasant origins, who was already singing the praises of her "natural garden" in the 1970s: "My idea of dying would be to sink just a bit deeper into the soil, to become part of my boundless hillside garden. Once it got used to my presence, my garden came to meet me, step by step, with great strides of rocks and trees."[47]

Notes: [38] *Monique Mosser, "Les dérives de l'idylle," p. 183–203, in* Le Jardin, notre double: sagesse et déraison *(Éditions Autrement, collection "Mutations," no 184, mars 1999), p. 185.* [39] *John Dixon Hunt,* The Picturesque Garden in Europe *(Thames & Hudson, 2003).* [40] *Helen Leach,* Cultivating Myths: Fiction, Fact and Fashion in Garden History *(Random House, New Zealand, 2000), p. 111. Her chapters "The Taming of the Wilderness" and "The Romantic Wild Garden" are rich in examples.* [41] *Gilles Clément, many books including* Le jardin en mouvement, Le jardin planétaire, Le domaine du Rayol. *Forthcoming:* Gilles Clément and the Planetary Garden *(Aubanel, 2006).* [42] *John Dixon Hunt, op. cit. His comments on current fashions are on pages 74, 89, 130 and 194-5.* [43] *Sir Joshua Reynolds quoted in John Dixon Hunt, p. 87.* [44] *Erik Borja,* Zen Gardens *(Seven Dials, 2001). Originally* Les leçons du jardin zen *(Le Chêne, 1999), p. 152.* [45] Le grand livre de la France sauvage, *editor Christian Bouchardy (Muséum national d'histoire naturelle, Bordas, 1998), p. 11.* [46] *Christian Tamisier, "La forêt en Provence: où sommes-nous et de quoi parle-t-on?" Contribution à une réflexion sur le rôle et les usages des bois et collines en basse Provence, photocopy document (CERFISE, April 1979), p. 20.* [47] *Marie Mauron,* Le printemps de la Saint-Martin *(Atelier Marcel Jullian, 1979), p. 17.*

Opposite upper left:
A moss garden at the home of designer Bruno Leroy.

Below:
The Picturesque mood can be created even in a tiny village courtyard.

Right:
The current fashion for tree houses can be linked to a taste for the Picturesque, here in the garden of Dominique Lafourcade.

Above left:
Giant boulders instead of a built wall in a garden by Jean Mus.

Right:
In a garden surrounding an old mill is a very contemporary *fabrique*: an electric train!

Ancient Landscapes

A Wine Estate in the Alpilles

Area: About 100 acres, of which about one third is vineyards, and 5 acres
are garden. Creators: Mr. and Mrs. Moatti (owners). Restored as of 1996.

_____ Two art collectors settling in the Alpilles hills
arranged their landscape in the grand Picturesque manner,
inspired by French and Italian art. The Domaine Dalmeran
already had definite advantages: hilly woodland mixed with
vineyards, a house built on the Palladian model sometime
after 1728 by Dame Marthe de Gras de Peigne (her tomb
can still be seen in the rustic chapel),[48] and fragments of a
Roman aqueduct strewn on the ground near the entrance
path, between huge boulders and the tortuous shapes of
Aleppo pines several hundred years old.

Notes: [48] *A detailed document on the history of the domain by Mr. and Mrs. Moatti is available on site for people visiting the winery.*

Notes : [49] *Quoted in Elizabeth Barlow Rogers,* Landscape Design: A Cultural and Architectural History *(Abrams, 2001), p. 240.*

Before coming to Dalmeran, Mr. and Mrs. Moatti owned a garden designed by Russell Page—valuable preparation for their new project. Mr. Moatti feels that "the effect of our landscape is such that everything else disappears." Certain views remind him of "pictures by Claude or Poussin." Everywhere gentle art was applied for natural effects. For example, opposite the house, existing groves of trees were shaped to enhance contrasts between neighboring planes, volumes, and foliage tones. A line of laurustinus was pruned lower than the olive crowns behind it and the taller evergreen oaks beyond, creating a layered composition which, seen from the house, gives depth to the view. The woodland has many "clearings." Near a marvelous viewpoint facing the sunset, clumps of wild box have been pruned into strange shapes that espouse rather than contradict their natural growth pattern. Elsewhere, an avenue of olive trees emerges from a wildflower tapestry. This has been baptized the "Renoir Walk."

At Dalmeran, thirty acres of vineyard and a thousand olive trees are surrounded by *garrigue* and pine woods. Transitions are carefully planned:

Boulders that were dug up when a new vineyard was planted were lined up along the edge of the new space to make a "Cyclopean wall," and lower branches on trees overlooking this scene were removed to let sunlight reach the vines. If certain eighteenth-century practitioners of the Picturesque hid agricultural activity, others allowed working landscapes to thrive at the heart of their most idyllic scenes, as is done here. The Dalmeran wine and olive oil both carry the prestigious label, AOC Les Baux-de-Provence.

All the essential ingredients of the Picturesque are present at Dalmeran: pleasantly rolling ground, cascading water, rough textures in tree trunks and stone, and long paths meandering through landscapes arranged like so many pictures for continuous discovery and varied moods. The vegetation is predominantly wild, but enrichment and pruning are both allowed. Viburnums, bay, box, broom, terebinths, thyme, rosemary, and several cistus all grow spontaneously, with asphodeles and aphyllantes on the highest hill. The park is big enough to include several types of soil and microclimates, and although the Moattis have not yet become botanists, they allow specialists to study their particularly rich flora. The only lawn is the large green swath linking the house to the wood. Pines nearby have been thinned to give more light to the undergrowth and to set off an ancient oak of great character. But in spite of a discreet electric fence, wild boar have made this grass their favorite playground. Luckily the Moattis are good friends with local hunters! Pheasant hunting is allowed, but other bird species are protected.

In landscaping, Italy remains the Moattis' great model. Visitors repaint the scenes according to their own visions: a specialist in Chinese gardens thought of the French painter Hubert Robert, while a French garden historian was reminded of China. English precedents also translate here into southern idiom. The following summary of the work of William Kent might equally apply to Dalmeran: attention to the tonality of vegetation and effects of perspective through contrasting light and dark foliage; expressive use of evergreens and other trees as screens and as a means of modulating otherwise vapid stretches of lawn; creation of both expectation and surprise by withholding choice prospects from immediate view, use of classical and antique structures to enliven the distant scene, juxtaposition of the working landscape with the idyllic.[49] Sometimes now, as then, the illusion created is so convincing that one forgets that a great landscape garden or gardened landscape is the result of hard work, as at Dalmeran, and is an art constantly renewed.

Contemporary Picturesque

Seafront Cliffs Near Marseille

Area: About 6 acres. Creators: Philippe Deliau and Juliette Hafteck (designers). Begun in 1997.

_____ In 1861, French Romantic writer George Sand wrote about the coast near this property: "Everything here is so picturesque, irregular, sweet, brusque, suave, vast and so full of contrasts that imagination can only paint it in the happiest colors."[50] A hundred years later, a Parisian bought this inlet between two high cliffs and replaced its château with a long, low house. Renovated today, almost invisible from the sea, it nestles into the curve of the valley and is, in the words of Frank Lloyd Wright, "not *on* the hill but *of* the hill."

Notes : [50]*George Sand, quoted in the catalogue for the exhibit: Méditerranée: De Courbet à Matisse, commissioner Françoise Cachin (Réunion des musées nationaux, 2000), p. 18.*

The slope still wears its original light woodland of cistus, junipers, terebinths, holly oaks and Aleppo pines, but a line of very old cypresses, like a row of sentinels, moves downhill to the west. On the eastern edge, a cascade tumbles along a rough, deep ravine past a small aqueduct and a stele, remnants of Art Deco architecture. History has left many traces here. It is said that Charles de Gaulle loved to walk in this wild wood.

The ALEP agency revived this perfect example of *rus in urbe* (countryside in the town), situated only five minutes away from a bustling town center. Near the entrance are vineyards and orchards carefully planted and tended by the new owners for their own use.

The valley retreat is invisible from the entrance plateau until you go right to the edge, expecting to find only the sea below. Philippe Deliau, founder of the ALEP agency, has long been a consultant at the nearby Domaine du Rayol, a park designed by Gilles Clément to reproduce Mediterranean biomes from all over the world. Deliau knows plants well, both wild and horticultural varieties. He mixes both here along winding paths, full of surprises, with crisscrossing sight lines and piquant contrasts of scale, from the massive forms of old trees to the finest details of light on foliage. Tall trees and old shrubs anchor the garden to its site. The stonework has been carefully restored and renewed—low retaining walls, short connecting

Above left:
A small open space for summer
festivities against the sublime
backdrop of the cliff.

Middle:
The house seems to melt into
the hillside.

Right:
The Art Deco aqueduct and
the ravine.

flights of steps. Every broad terrace is like a showcase. One example, near the bottom of the hill, uses *Clematis armandii* as a ground cover around a stand of Mexican orange (*Choisya*) with heavenly bamboo (*Nandina*) against a mass of acanthus and ivy. All of these are tough, drought-resistant plants. Farther up, another planting mixes bottle brush, ballotas, euphorbias, coronillas and shrubby germander set among waves of muehlenbeckia. Here and there a bit of wall shows through, echoing the stone house perched above. Certain oaks and Judas trees which have self-sown in many places are pruned to let light through their branches and show up the beauty of their trunks. Others become screens or a pivot where the path branches. Seen from the rim of the valley above, the terraces themselves look like the waves of a green sea. Footpaths across the hillside are invisible from any distance, with the exception of one central path, marked by a low myrtle hedge. A lovely addition to the scene is the decking in exotic wood (from a fair trade source) supported by chestnut spikes that now accompanies the cascade on its downward plunge. From this walkway, one can look down on a mix of black ophiopogon and golden bamboos, a collection of tree ferns (*Dickensonia*), and hostas, all rather unexpected in a southern French garden and maintained in good health thanks to artificial mist-makers hidden in nearby trees.

Acclimatizing exotic plants is, after all, an old Riviera tradition.

The owners, designers, and gardener all love this place. It is also a garden for living—running down to the beach, playing *pétanque* in the shaded court, swimming in the pool that juts out over the ravine, or admiring the view from the rooftop solarium. But only the gardener, Guilherm Cognet, knows the most intimate pleasures of the place, as he picks ivy from the heart of a cycad, prunes the terebinths into cushions, guides white lantanas as they spill over the walls. Some paths not planned at the start have been made to accommodate his favorite walks. He feels at ease with the resident fauna, but he has a great advantage—the closeness of the town protects this property from wild boar. A happy Robinson Crusoe, Cognet loves spending his days in this narrow valley under the high cliff, pervaded by the incessant murmur of the sea.

Working Woodland

An Eighteenth-Century Domain Near Aix

Area: Garden about 4.5 acres, plus vineyards and olive orchards.
Creators: the owners, Anthony Archer Wills (water garden expert),
Claus Scheinert (horticultural designer), Laurence Berlemont of the
Cabinet d'agronomie provençale (agricultural advisor), Bruno and
Alexandre Lafourcade (architectural restoration). Begun around 1990.

_____ Émile de Girardin, friend and patron of French
eighteenth-century philosopher Jean-Jacques Rousseau, wrote
that "a successful garden should allow visitors to enjoy a series
of different landscapes, without ever letting their interest flag.
Scenes should include the always lively spectacle of working
farmland."[51] At Le Canadel, east of Aix-en-Provence, an
industrious Australian couple has been creating such an
ideal garden around an eighteenth-century *bastide*.

Notes: [51] *Émile de Girardin, "De la composition des paysages, ou des moyens d'embellir la nature autour des habitations, en y joignant l'agréable à l'utile," (1777) quoted by* Michel Baridon, *Les Jardins: paysagistes, jardiniers, poètes (Robert Lafont, 1998), p. 903.*

Michel Baridon, a historian specializing in that period, suggests that the mix of landscape beauty and productivity may belong to Protestant tradition. In fact, it has been characteristic of Mediterranean life for millennia. The Roman villas of Pliny the Younger were often cited as examples in the eighteenth century and still are today.

Le Canadel is a genuine Provençal working *bastide*, but as it exists today, it also resembles the northern French *fermes ornées* (ornamental farms) of Rousseau's time. Whatever its heritage,

its owners work very hard. He cuts down trees to clear land, and she carts off the fallen trunks with her tractor. She also loves to prune olive trees, which is just as well as they have added over eight hundred new ones, punctuated by sixty cypresses placed for elegant contrast. This much planting does need professional help, however, and the owners have brought in an agency that specializes in the management of agricultural lands attached to vacation homes, a new market in Provence.

When they bought this property, the Australians were looking for an authentic *bastide* with the

traditional, majestic plane trees and lots of water. The house they found sits half way down the slope of a broad, wild valley and was restored for contemporary elegance and comfort by the Lafourcade family. To the west is a wooded hillside with giant Aleppo pines and white oaks. To the north and the east, old terracing now repaired has provided space for new orchards and vineyards. Southwest, out of sight of the house, a lavender field stretches by a row of old stone beehives built on site. Beyond is a belvedere, under the high crowns of pines, used for playing *boules* and valuable as a fire break. These various landscapes are not only arranged as a series of admirable pictures but are also spaces defined by use, each with its own.

Water is dramatically present in each, staged by the English specialist, Anthony Archer Wills. The scenes he has created could almost be called a series of aquatic *fabriques* in the eighteenth century tradition. Just inside the entrance gate is an elegant cascade; farther up the hill are three small pools covered in May with fragrant *Aponeton distachyos*, and farther on is a series of rustic fountains. East of the house Wills imagined an artificial lake, which, though brand-new, also appears to date from the eighteenth century. Covering more than an acre, it is called Lake Antoine in his honor. The serenity of this artificial landscape, enhanced by four sculpted urns marking the main sight lines, gives no hint of the hard work needed to make it. Wills remembers long days in the July heat when he, the owners, and a handful of workmen soldered together the black plastic liner. The water that feeds this lake comes from nine springs uphill,

only yards away, their stone wellheads surrounded by an old wall. Where does the water end up? Wills replies, "Where it always did, at the bottom of the hill. We just make it work a bit on the way down."

More ornamental fountains surround the *bastide*, included in a formal layout of mixed borders with a rose parterre. These spaces were designed by Claus Scheinert, of the famous Casella gardens in Opio. The olive orchards are under-planted with wildflowers, mixing spontaneous growth with professional sowings. The various experts consulted by the owners of this property are both local and exotic, like the varieties planted. Even the head gardener is a specialist: He first learned botany with the famous Marcel Kroenlien of the Jardin exotique de Monaco, a friend of his father's.

Unsuspected by passersby outside, this hidden valley is much loved by its new residents. They savor its seasons because where they live in Australia, they say, there are only two, not four. They are proud of bringing new life to this land, reviving its many historic vestiges, aware that their plantations (seven more acres of vineyard added in 2003) will not benefit their own children but strangers. They generously contribute a store of energy and good humor for the benefit of future generations.

Horticultural "High Tech"

An Architect's Retreat in the Var

Area: Roughly a third of an acre, dropping 80 to 90 feet to the sea.
Creators: Rick Mather (architect), aided by Jean-Laurent Félizia (gardenist).
Begun in 1998.

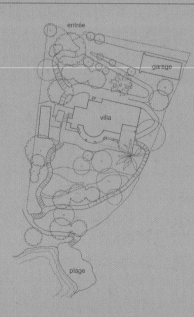

Rick Mather is a London-based architect whose projects have included the Wallace Collection, the headquarters and Lindley Library of the Royal Horticultural Society, the South Bank Centre, and many other museums, theaters, galleries, university complexes, and restaurants. His style has been called "sensual high-tech," but in fact he often is required to adapt his contemporary "minimalism" to historic properties.

For his own holiday home on the Var coast, he chose a villa built in 1937 in a mode he deems "rather romantic." He simplified its spaces to provide more immediate access to the outdoors. Above all, he added a wide deck that gives the impression that you can reach out and touch the sea below. Lunch is often taken there, even in winter.

When Mather was eleven years old, he helped his father build a house in the Oregon forest. He describes his mother's wildflower garden as an "outdoor room," a projection of living space into the landscape in a manner that juxtaposed formal simplicity with untamed nature. His property in the Var creates a similar effect. The house is set partway down a slope to the sea, one story high to the north, two to the south. From the entrance, the hillside seems to flow downward to engulf it in the manner of Frank Lloyd Wright. From below, it recalls Le Corbusier's white villa floating above the landscape, with the deck as a kind of hanging garden. The steep grade lets the architect achieve seemingly opposite effects with one house.

The luxuriant plantings surrounding the house include both indigenous and exotic species, a harmony maintained by Jean-Laurent Félizia, himself a native and founder of the studio Mouvements et paysages (p. 68). From the outset, Mather and Félizia took pains to retain as many pre-existing plants as possible, including some magnificent trees: two eucalyptus, a tall cypress, two Canary date palms, several cork oaks and acacias, and a fine sophora. Mather began by simply "editing" the landscape—shaping trees in a natural way to enhance the rhythm of their trunks, their architecture, and their natural growth. In other places, he edited to frame views using wind-bent trunks that became part of the picture themselves. In this way, a series of visual and sensual experiences was organized along the visitors' walk through the garden. Regular upkeep is necessary to ensure the illusion of spontaneity. The necessary human intervention (mainly pruning and weeding) must remain discreet, if not invisible.

The garden easily separates into two parts, above and below the house, which are linked by winding flights of steps a bit like bridges on a ship. The north section is dominated by a beautiful grove of *Arbutus unedo*, restored and lightly shaped for sculptural effect. Many treasures have been tucked into the low terracing which surrounds these trees: a *Marsetella moquiniana* from the Canary Island and an *Erica bauera* with white and pink flowers, for example. The steepest parts have been colonized by bulbs, such as dark blue flowering Algerian iris, Bulgarian iris, and wild freesias.

Below the house, winding paths unveil the panorama in successive stages. They lead off toward the beach on the east side under the shade of an enormous cork oak with three massive trunks. They come back up on the west side, where more open, sunny space seems brightly exotic with its clumps of euryops and South African osteospermums. You never retrace your steps but are kept moving from one view to the next. Neighbors are well hidden though close by. The eastern ravine is edged with old yuccas, cactus, agaves, bamboos, and a hedge of naturalized *Acacia dealbata*. To the west, wire fencing will soon disappear under a cloud of exuberant, scented Burmese honeysuckle (*Lonicera hilde-brandiana*). Mather hates bare ground: Everything must swarm. Not just any plant will do, however, and smilax has become public enemy number one. Félizia likes to experiment with weed-suppressing ground covers on these banks, which easily erode, and appreciates the Australian species *Myoporum*. Whatever their origin, plants must resist drought and poor soil. There are no cascades here; the sea suffices with its moods, its murmurs, and its constantly renewed energy.

This garden offers an intimate, welcoming, and hospitable version of the Picturesque. Even on this small scale, it plays a good deal on the "intricacy" admired in the eighteenth century, a quality defined by landscape architect Uvedale Price as "that disposition of objects which, by a partial and uncertain concealment, excites and nourishes curiosity."[52] But one could also cite as a precursor, for his own mixtures of contemporary architecture and exuberant plantings, Brazilian designer Roberto Burle Marx.

Notes: [52] *A key quotation in Elizabeth Barlow Rogers,* Landscape Design: A Cultural and Architectural History *(Abrams, 2001), p. 254, and also in John Dixon Hunt, op. cit., p. 76.*

Romantic Exoticism

A Town Emporium at L'Isle-sur-la-Sorgue

Area: Roughly a quarter acre. Creator: Michel Biehn (owner).
Begun in 1990.

———— Eighteenth-century French gardens were often designed as "invitations to flights of exotic fancy and imaginary voyages."[53] The nineteenth-century French Romantic Théophile Gautier wrote, "Style and fantasy, far from being futile concerns, are surely essential ingredients for any measure of happiness."[54]

Notes : [53] *Monique Mosser,* op. cit., *p. 183.* [54] *See* Michel Biehn's Healthy Recipes: International Cuisine from a Provençal Table *(Flammarion, 2003),* op. cit., *p. 14.*

Opposite:
Pots of all sizes, here grouped around the summer lilac, allow for endless experimenting.

Above, left to right:
Biehn's elder son made this whirlwind paving while the younger, still a child, grows strawberries in this miniature garden. A wisteria creates an intimate link between house and garden.

Following pages:
The Picturesque in a town garden contrasts stone and plants, precious exotics with nature's own gifts. At the bottom of the garden is the River Sorgue.

In our time, Michel Biehn espouses both traditions, though he champions an art of living rather than art for art's sake. He lives at L'Isle-sur-la-Sorgue (a town famous for its antiques markets), where he is one of the leading lights. His business card presents him as a *magicien de maisons* (magician designer). Like Gautier and his fellow poets, Biehn admires both aristocratic elegance and genuine grassroots folk art but spurns the middle-level, bourgeois style as boring at best.

Nonetheless, the house he bought for his family in the heart of town is a solid, middle-class home. It was built in the late eighteenth century by a tradesman whose fortune came from the weaving and selling of wool. In this style of house, the rooms are all too much alike for Biehn's taste, so he has transformed each into a different port of call or another chapter in a tale by Scheherazade. Customers of the Biehn emporium may visit the ground floor and thus discover treasures he

brings back from Asia and the Middle East, as well as those from his native Provence. Already as a child, Biehn loved both his home and far-flung destinations. His mother was the daughter of a Provençal poet and his father was a government official constantly posted in new places.

Both the front and back gardens, in proper bourgeois style, are extensions of the residence. The public visits only the front one but can glimpse the back from windows above. The gardens too have various moods, solitary in the early morning when Biehn enjoys a walk accompanied only by friendly blackbirds. But for entertaining on warm summer evenings, a small dance floor in the back garden is outlined in floating, colored lamps for a very Impressionist effect.

Enclosed for privacy on both sides, the garden opens onto the Sorgue River, its dazzling waters half screened by stands of bamboo. Bridges, a favorite feature of Picturesque gardens, are rare

Visitors wander at will through a series of half-hidden spaces, each with its own character, from the long pergola to the little vegetable garden edged with marigolds and bronze-leafed fennel. Sight lines cross and get caught up in the ever-changing play of light and shade. Transitions are marked by changes in the paving. The flowering shrubs are those one finds in traditional family gardens: Persian lilac, philadelphus, hibiscus, choisya, hortensia, "Banks" roses. Instead of Romantic woodland copses, there are miniature groves and clearings with a few tables and chairs scattered here and there throughout the garden. Here, as in the house, no space has a single, fixed function. This ambiguity is already an encouragement to imaginary voyages.

Colors are soft here, except for bright yellows around the little vegetable plot. This is an old-fashioned Provençal "green garden" with seasonal floral highlights, never very many at once. It is a golden garden also, thanks to the palms, the bamboos, the underside of the thick magnolia leaves. Box and laurustinus contribute solid shapes and dark lines, screens, and curtains. But everything lights up in summer thanks to the sophisticated staging of white flowers in pots, treasures Biehn brings back from the Carpentras market: cosmos, gauras, dahlias, daturas, lantanas. This bedding out also lets him experiment with his spaces and make discoveries, so that the garden remains dynamic, never staid. He is not much interested in the names of his plants and explains, "What motivates me is not knowledge but sensuous encounter." In this regard, he echoes another precursor, philosopher Jean-Jacques Rousseau, for whom "the man of taste lives for living and knows how to enjoy his own company."[55]

in today's parks, but Michel Biehn's small family garden, in the heart of town, has two.

What makes this garden mysterious, even when seen from above, are the trees. The oldest are about two hundred years old: a linden, a *Magnolia grandiflora*, a summer lilac (*Lagerstroemia indica*) with several trunks and bright purple-pink flowers. There is also a little collection of palm trees, an exotic feature common in nineteenth-century town gardens in Provence. Two majestic plane trees succumbed to blight, a loss so strongly felt that the family nearly moved away. Marc Nucera has transformed one into a massive sculpture, a kind of Romantic ruin. The low stump of the second tree has become an altar to Shiva, half-smothered now by a mix of Provençal reeds (*Arundo donax*) and sunchokes.

Notes : **55** *Jean-Jacques Rousseau,* Julie, ou, la nouvelle Héloïse, *IVe partie (Gallimard, collection La Pléiade, 1964), p. 482. Philip Stewart and Jean Vaché, in* Julie, or, the New Heloise *(University Press of New England, 1997, p. 393–394) translate this slightly differently:* "a man of taste ...who lives to live, knows how to enjoy his own being."

Sculpted landscapes

"Designs for the twenty-first century," writes historian Janet Waymark, "bind together art, sculpture, and Land Art at all levels from domestic gardens to larger landscapes."[56] Land Art as practiced today in Provence no longer stresses entropy and destruction, as did the American movement of the 1970s, nor has it submitted to pastiche and derision as in the postmodern era which followed.[57] In today's version, growth counts as much as decay. Young artists involve the whole round of life and death, of movement and energy—a cycle deeply familiar to gardeners everywhere. Marc Nucera, sculpting a dead hundred-year-old pine, invaded by other species, imagines its thoughts: "My body now feeds myriad forms of new life [. . .] I die and live again in so many different ways"[58] (see page 100). One of these ways is art—even if only for a time.

The balance between artwork, place, and duration is crucial for artists working outdoors today. Nucera usually works on living trees *in situ*, foreseeing their natural habit and future growth in his design. One of his models is British artist Andy Goldsworthy, whose creations can be as ephemeral as rain shadows or as lasting as stone cairns (see p. 262–263). Goldsworthy considers that "there is a difference between placing and making a work on a site. A work made in a place grows there and becomes part of it in a way that a sited object has difficulty in achieving."[59] He writes elsewhere:

> At times it is difficult to say where my touch ends and the place begins. This lack of division can at times be disturbing. It is easier and in some ways more pleasing to make a sculpture work through its contrast to the surroundings, but the greater challenge is to make work that is completely welded to its site.

Provençal landscapes lend themselves particularly well to such dialogues, because it is often difficult to tell where spontaneous rock

formations end and human constructions begin.

Like sculpture, a house may stand out from or melt into its setting. English designer Russell Page wondered how he would garden round one of Le Corbusier's "suspended buildings," which appeared to "strain away from their surroundings like complicated box-kites scarcely tethered by a string." He discovered the answer on the roof of Le Corbusier's studio, where the architect "had been content to spread earth and, as he said, leave the birds and the wind to do the rest." The result was "a wild and haphazard growth from seeds blown there by the wind or left by birds."[60] In Provence today, one often sees such contrasts between minimalist architecture

and wild settings. Sometimes this opposition is the point, but on other sites, Land Art weaves unexpected connections between the house and its surroundings, establishing subtle dialogue.

For today's generation, architecture and sculpture overlap more and more. You can often walk inside today's Land Art, even sleep in it! (See p. 263.) Painting—the garden designer's model from the eighteenth-century Picturesque through to the twentieth-century's carefully composed borders—has been left behind. Artists today prefer process to objects, space to images, participation rather than spectatorship. And yet it is sculpture rather than architecture that provides the new model. Erik Borja, a landscape sculptor from the Drôme, explains:

The traditional formal garden was an extension of human space, designed by man, marked by the presence of man:

that's architecture. Sculpture means complete freedom. It has no reference to anything outside itself. It's a free electron. Architecture is inextricably linked to geometry, to mathematics, sculpture not at all. Its harmony emerges from chaos, whereas architecture and chaos cannot mix. Architecture has rules, if only so that walls won't fall down.[61]

Formalism is often interpreted as an attempt to control the environment. Andy Goldsworthy reacts to this cliché with his usual good sense:

My approach to the earth began as a reaction against geometry. I used to think it an arrogance imposed upon nature, and still do. But I've also realized that it is arrogance to think man invented geometry. As regards my own work, I'd like to think geometry has

appeared in it to the same degree I have found it in nature.... Having said all this, I am always suspicious of geometry, cautious in using it. This last year saw my first use of the spiral. It's taken me a long time to come to terms with this form, so evident in nature. I still avoid the overblown spiral. I prefer that of the unfolding fern, which gives the impression of endless growth, or of the simple ammonite in stone.[62]

Living sculpture in Provence has traditionally meant clipped greenery. Southern broadleaf evergreen shrubs lend themselves to pruning, while Mediterranean light brings out contrasts in forms and volumes, creating effects that are sculptural. Northerners sometimes attribute clipping to a desire to impose human domination on wild nature. Belgian landscape architect René Péchère loved to remind romantic souls that nothing is more "natural" than cutting one's fingernails![63] Provençal farmers who have practiced "sustainable" agriculture for centuries know that fruit trees and vines quickly die if left unpruned—as do roses. Human intervention in

such cases is a form of partnership. Who could aspire to control in a climate famous for sudden frosts, heat waves, floods, droughts, and fires? When novelist Colette settled in Saint-Tropez in 1928, she dreamt of "disheveled roses," and would not allow her gardener to plant anything in straight rows. Two years later, she concluded that her rejection of all formality was a mistake in the Mediterranean world, a lack of "true *savoir-vivre*."[64]

The Mediterranean has always blended wild nature with formal elements in ways that appeal to today's designers, tired of conventional categorizing. The new Land Art, like the new Picturesque and Romantic styles, assimilates garden and landscape, but attributes an entirely different role to human intervention. In the Picturesque, this must remain hidden like the garden's very boundaries, melting into their surroundings. Land Artists proudly assert human interaction with the natural setting, whether in boundless landscape or the enclosed space of a garden. After all, gardners are also human beings experimenting with life-giving energies in hopes of creating formal coherence, however ephemeral. Size makes no difference.

Nicole de Vésian laid out a small bed of lavender, alternating pruned globes and free-flowering plants for a sculpted tapestry effect. Land Artist Henri Olivier imagined a modest vegetable garden in the form of a spiral. Rémy Duthoit makes wind sculptures. Bruno Leroy makes mossy "landscapes" in wooden boxes, and decorated his tiny Japanese garden with dandelion garlands. Outdoor art—formal, wild, or a blend of both; boundless or miniature; transitory or durable— is perhaps merely one way in which the human animal marks his territory.

Notes: [56] *Janet Waymark,* Modern Garden Design: Innovation since 1900 *(Thames & Hudson, 2003), p. 7.* [57] *European accounts of American Land Art include Gilles A. Tiberghien,* Nature, art, paysage *(Actes Sud, 2002) and Udo Weilacher,* Between Landscape Architecture and Land Art *(Birkhäuser, 1996). For a French view of postmodern derision, see Anne Caquelin,* Petit traité du Jardin ordinaire *(Payot et Rivages, 2003) and* Petit traité d'art contemporain *(Seuil, 1996).* [58] *Unpublished poem by Nucera composed in homage to this tree.* [59] *Andy Goldsworthy,* Time *(Thames & Hudson, 2000), p. 22.* [60] *Russell Page,* Education of a Gardener *(The Harvill Press, 1995), p. 266.* [61] *Erik Borja, telephone interview with the author.* [62] *Andy Goldsworthy,* Hand to Earth: Andy Goldsworthy Sculpture, 1976–1990, *ed. Terry Friedman and Andy Goldsworthy (Harry N. Abrams, 1990), p. 162.* [63] *René Péchère,* Jardins dessinés: Grammaires des jardins *(Éditions de l'atelier urbain, 1987), p. 120.* [64] *Colette,* Prisons et paradis *(Fayard, 1986), p. 59.*

Living in the Woods

A Contemporary House Near Uzès

Area: 1 acre. Creators: François Privat (architect),
Sandrine Cnudde (designer), Marc Nucera (Land Artist), Angel Cao (botanist).
Begun in January 2000.

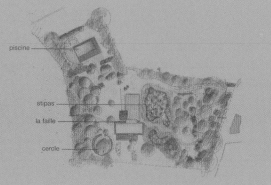

A city couple took in hand this lightly wooded abandoned farmland that had been in her family for over fifty years. Themselves descendants of distinguished architects, these owners wanted to avoid nostalgia and build for their own time. They chose François Privat, a well-known architect in Uzès, who says he responded to their "need for space, volume, and light." The house has two parts—one vertical, one horizontal—with large, ribbon windows framing both nearby woodland and the medieval town.

Seen from the front, the building seems raised on stilts, but viewed from the steep hill above, it looks well-rooted in the ground. Minimalist in style, it stands surrounded by wild woodland. At first this seems a deliberate contrast, like the roof garden of Le Corbusier's studio as described by Russell Page (p. 134). Closer examination reveals that two young artists have created strong connections between building and site.

The owners had at first imagined nothing more than a completely spontaneous, natural setting—not a garden at all. Then Sandrine Cnudde, who had already designed wild spaces for chef Michel Bras (famous for his cooking with local plants in the remote Aubrac region),

spoke to them about "the true identity of the land, linked to its natural development." Cnudde intended simply to shape the spontaneous vegetation, "to open it up a bit." To anchor the house on the street side and give it "a gently playful air," she planted a carpet of stipas out of which arise colorful mobile sculptures (works of a Dutch artist whose *nom de guerre* is Mike Delight). For the rest, she began to feel a need for stronger connections between the building and the woods. She understood that creative pruning would be required to make this happen.

At this point, fate brought her into contact with Marc Nucera, a "sculptor of living plants" in the words of his admirer, Christine Picasso.

Marc trained at the agricultural colleges of Carpentras and Châteauneuf-du-Rhône before inventing a new specialty: "landscape pruning." This, he explains, involves working with a tree to encourage its natural development in connection with its setting. An admirer of Brancusi and Goldsworthy, he learned a great deal from working closely with such fine artists as Nicole de Vésian and Alain-David Idoux (p. 42, 51, 144, and 154).

Nucera's trees often mark transitions, points where diverse energies meet. For example, to connect the outer angle of the southern terrace with an ancient pine tree, he imagined a simple circle of stones that leads the eye first toward neighboring tree trunks, then up to the sky.

Another work was inspired by looking from above, especially at the almost transparent staircase connecting the two big rectangular volumes of the house. The architect had called this connection a *faille* (fault, in the geological sense). Nucera, unprompted, thought of the same word. He imagined prolonging this line with a row of large white stones found on site, in the manner of English earth artist Richard Long. Far from seeming imposed on the land, this work looks like a projection from underground. The owners see it as the "backbone of an emerging monster." This simple gesture transforms house and land into parts of the same, vast landscape sculpture. Like a white arrow, it also directs the eye to the plateau

Opposite:
The transparent "fault" connecting
the two parts of the house.

Above:
The alliance of architecture
and garden.

Following pages:
The carpet of stipas with mobiles by
Mike Delight, seen from above and
from ground level. The sculpted
landscape allows for crossing
sight lines. Today, plants are
preferred that move with changing
weather and evolve with the
seasons, like grasses and
deciduous trees.

above where a large olive orchard offers splendid views on the surrounding patchwork of fields.

Nucera and Cnudde, working harmoniously with enthusiastic owners, keep discovering and innovating. Their inspiration comes directly from the site itself, which they explore and see anew on each visit. Nature remains free, rough, multiform, vital, constantly changing. The house remains smooth, firm, and strong, though its walls lend themselves to shifting patterns of light and shadow. "Taken as a whole," says Sandrine Cnudde, "this is a place which hangs on to the earth."

Nucera admires Francis Bacon, and has adapted from him the idea that true knowledge emerges from the nuances and harmonies between simple forms with limited differences. The quest for this subtle equilibrium makes Nucera "pursue the image and confer coherence on separate parts." François Privat, the architect, is delighted with the partnership of these two young artists. On the flat roof of his house has been placed not a garden but the massive, gnarled stump of an uprooted tree. The whole team finds this an appropriate symbol of how site memory, through natural evolution, can be experienced as art.

Agricultural Land Art

An Old Farmstead in the Alpilles

Area: About 20 acres. Creators: Alain David Idoux (designer), Hugues Bosc
(architect), Marc Nucera (Land Artist), and Natacha Guillaumont (consultant designer).
Property purchased in 1993, garden begun in 1997, Death of Alain David Idoux, 1999.

Alain-David Idoux, a self-designated "sculptor of
landscapes" (p. 42, 51, and 154), created his masterpiece
on this austere site facing the silver crags of the Alpilles
hills. As a child the current owner used to picnic here and
fell in love with its exceptional panorama. He and his wife,
both modern art collectors, wanted a design that would melt
seamlessly into these spectacular surroundings. Idoux first
planted trees on the northern rise behind the house as a
windbreak. Loosely grouped, mixing local species, these
groves today look completely natural, in spite of the artful
shaping of their trunks and crowns.

Close to the house, Idoux designed small terraces and large planter boxes which, seen from indoors, frame the spectacular views beyond. Each aspect of the house has a different arrangement of planes and volumes leading the eye toward the horizon. The practical function of each space counts also, of course, but less than this magic visual unfolding. When you visit, no one direction dominates, and there are no single viewpoints from which to appreciate prearranged tableaux. Whichever way you go, you make the garden happen as you walk. For example, a triangular field of lavender has rows converging on an obelisk, beyond which rises a medieval hilltown. As you arrive from the parking lot, it first looks like an ordinary rectangular field punctuated by old almond trees. As you continue, its shape is gradually revealed, always in perspective and with balanced proportions, like the movement of a kaleidoscope. The transitions are continuous and harmonious, with no dead spaces.

Throughout the garden, there are several such "sculpted landscapes" that change as you

Opposite:
A "green room," made from
a natural grove of local oaks
(Quercus ilex), seen from
outside and in.

Following pages:
The stone river and the
almond spiral.

Notes: [65] *Idoux, quoted in
Page Dickey,* Breaking Ground
(New York, Artisan, 1997), p. 100.

little plants that blend into the light woodland. Here is one of several "green rooms"—half open spaces carved out of holly oak groves. A secret footpath leads from here to a river of stones and cacti, where another obelisk points to distant silver peaks.

Each arrangement makes use of local materials and common plants that are either native or naturalized. Nothing is mannered or extravagant. The range of species is however broader than one might think at first glance. The owner keeps a detailed electronic plant list in a pocket near his heart.

Sculpture, landscape … may one in fact speak of a garden at all? The owner's wife insists that the word garden is too "restrictive" for this place. She claims that Idoux, like his clients, preferred minimalism to decoration. Nor are his inspirations preconceived designs merely laid on the landscape, just as easily transposed elsewhere. Marc Nucera, who trained with Idoux, admires in his work "that perfect internalization of faraway scenery into something personal and intimate." This is a stronger phenomenon than the borrowing of landscape so often attributed to Japanese design, though Idoux's work, because it mixes free forms and pruning, is often compared to Asian models. His agricultural geometries transformed into metaphysical vision also recall the work of Spanish designer Fernando Caruncho, who has seen and admired this property. Idoux wanted his clients and their visitors to feel the deepest resonances of a place on which his art confers a dimension not limited to art alone. "It is important," he used to say, "that everything we create has a meaning."[65]

pass. Visitors must be in motion to appreciate them fully; they must actively participate and pay careful attention. Some of the best effects are so discreet that visitors sometimes ask, "Where is the garden?" The exchanges between land, eye, mind, and heart are all the richer for being subtle.

Each arrangement may be admired close up, from inside, and from a distance: the lavender triangle, the three low terraces of the Grass Garden situated between house and meadow, the olive tree avenue which leads straight to the Secret Garden with its magnificent walnut tree. Off to one side is a vast spiral of almond trees, a contour outlined with dazzling white limestone pebbles. Close to the house, waves of mixed cistus varieties lead to a swimming pool nestled into the rock and surrounded by a mosaic of

Japanese Miniature

In a Mountain Château Park

Area: 8,600 square feet. Creators: Erik Borja (inside a park originally
laid out by Alain-David Idoux, Pierre Baud (technical advisor).
Begun in 2002.

_____ Born in Algiers, Erik Borja has lived since 1979
in the Rhone valley on the northern edge of Provence. His
admiration for Asian gardens began on a trip to Japan,
where he discovered oriental "mastery of reduced scale, of
limited space, of framing, artifice, and subjectivity."[66] Borja
trained as a sculptor at the Paris Beaux-Arts academy
but today works mainly as a landscape designer. His own
garden, Les Clermonts, blends Asian and Mediterranean
inspiration, embracing an entire landscape.

Notes: [66] *Erik Borja, Zen Gardens (Seven Dials, 2001). Originally Les Leçons du Jardin zen (Le Chêne, 1999), p. 8.*
Translation here by Louisa Jones.

Some years ago, Alain-David Idoux designed for this château park near Mont Ventoux a series of scenes based on squares and circles, symbols for him of heaven and earth. More recently, after Idoux passed away, the owners engaged Borja to design a steep slope, half wooded, which links areas just below the château to open spaces outside. Borja preferred to isolate this site from the rest of the park in order to create a "place where you can lose yourself completely and forget everything around you." His part is open only to the north, in order, he explains, "to frame the view onto a nearby vineyard, distant fields, and untamed woodland on the local mountain beyond." He let the site itself determine the new garden's layout. His conception respects the three conditions of Japanese gardening as he sees them: the *no-suji* (the site's lines of force), the *tayori* (metaphysical structure of the

spaces), and the *fuzeï* (dynamic, poetic spirit). Nonetheless, the ground was considerably modified before the garden could be laid out. Borja explains, "I don't work with a hammer and chisel but with a bulldozer. This is what sets me off from most garden designers, who are horticulturalists interested in composing pictures. For me, the main thing is earth and rock, and the plants come after, like hair on a head."[67]

It all began, then, with the placing of stones and boulders brought from as far away as the Vercors. The owner and Borja went together to choose them and returned with four big truckloads. Several attempts were needed to half bury each rock in just the right place "to create the effect of a minor landslide, an impression of instability but also of dynamism generated by the play of surfaces and angles."[68]

Next came water: an irregular cascade set off by miniature islands, lanterns, and of course a

Notes: [67] *Erik Borja, telephone interview with the author.* [68] *Erik Borja, op. cit., p. 63.* [69] *Erik Borja, telephone interview with the author.*

154

Above, left to right:
Garden details, including the covered walkway and the ablution stone. As Erik Borja explains, "It would be useless to plant in our regions, which have such different climates, the same species of plants as in Japan. It is by careful observation of the ecosystem and climate, the quality of local water, the hydrometrics of the air and the nature of the soil that one can select plants and trees suitable for any chosen site."

Following pages:
According to Borja, "Japanese gardens are deliberately artificial; the result is a re-creation of nature, not its restoration for the sake of preservation."

stone for ablutions. A small covered walkway makes it possible to admire the scene from a sheltered place. It is a fixed point from which to discover a garden constantly in flux according to the weather, the hour, or the season. The effect sought here is not the timelessness of Zen gardens, but a sense of impressions ever-changing throughout the year. Plants are important because their growth embodies this evolution so well, as it is connected to cosmic order. Borja insists, however, on that "complete absence of the anecdotal, that paring down which allows the spectator to escape the reality around him and to take flight in meditation and dream."

Borja describes the result as living sculpture: "In other words, as volumes in space which play on light and shade. It is also a work which fits into its setting. This is essential in Japanese gardening, where a creation must never draw

attention like a wart on a nose."[69] The owners also comment that the gardens look as if they had always been there. This is not to imply that the château might have once had a Japanese owner! Rather this remark acknowledges a happy harmony between new contours and old, between proportions, planes, frames, and volumes, which the setting seems to welcome as its own. The plantings too are mainly composed of Mediterranean species that grow well here but can look Japanese: myrtles, terebinths, cistus, rosemary, and Aleppo pines.

For the owners, this garden is above all an expression of beauty in which art becomes spirit. A creation inspired by Buddhism is thus added to the others in the château park, which subtly evoke all of the world's religions.

Symbolic Quests

The Alchemist's Gardens and the Noria Gardens

Area: Alchemist's Gardens: 2 acres by 1 acre; Noria Gardens: 1 acre.
Creators: Éric Ossart (designer) and Arnaud Maurières (designer).
Alchemist's Gardens begun in 1995, open since 1999;
la Noria begun in 2000, open since 2004.

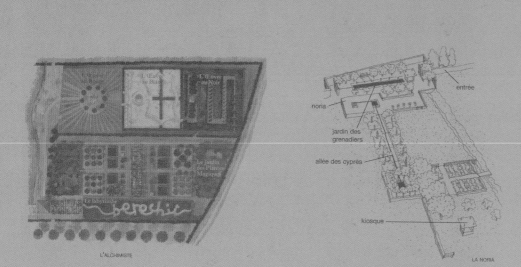

Éric Ossart and Arnaud Maurières, Mediterranean by their origins and their affinities, range in their work from purely mineral Land Art to bright floral carpets of annuals.

They consider that sculpting the landscape is a way of "worshiping nature by turning it into art." To be successful however, a project must be "seen as a whole from the garden's conception."[70] Where the site is historic, the aim is to "convert remnants of the past into new myths." In recent years, this approach produced controversial gardens at the Musée de Cluny in Paris and, in the south, these two fascinating and very different examples. At the Alchemist's Gardens near the hilltown of Eygalières, everything began with a mysterious detail in the sculpted façade of a manor house that dates from 1572; in the Noria Gardens, near Uzès west of the Rhone, the starting point was an ancient water pumping system belonging to an eighteenth-century manor house.

Both domains are privately owned but open to the public under certain conditions. The Mas de la Brune, site of the Alchemist's Gardens, was already a small luxury hotel in 1995 when it was purchased by the Larouzière family (landowners and art patrons for generations). At the Mas du Licon, the Deparis family had already fixed up luxury bed and breakfast accommodations before even thinking about creating the Noria Gardens. In both cases, the projects suggested by Maurières and Ossart caught the imagination of the owners, appealing to their curiosity and their senses. Both gardens became the focus for cultural activities involving the public. The

Notes: [70] *Arnaud Maurières et Éric Ossart,* Jardins nomades: Tapis de fleurs *(Édisud, 1997);* Jardins de voyage: 20 leçons de paysage *(Édisud, 1999);* Paradise Gardens *(Le Chêne, 2001). Translantions here by Louisa Jones.* [71] *Quotation taken from the explanatory material provided on site.*

Above, left to right:
The Black Square, reign of Saturn, has lead and gravel paving, hornbeam and black oaks, and a square dark pool.

Following pages:
The theatrical curtains separating the Botanical and Alchemy Gardens; entrance to the White Square and its display of "Iceberg" roses mixed with gauras and striped *Miscanthus sinensis*; two views of the botanic garden of Magic Plants with its live willow hedging.

Larouzières founded Hortus, an association that organizes, with the help of the local township, an annual conference on ethnobotany. The Deparis founded another association, Artists in Gardens, to sponsor a colloquium on eighteenth-century follies and *fabriques*.

The gardens at the Mas de la Brune occupy two long rectangular fields once used for growing spring vegetables, and bordered with thick cypress windbreaks. Their layout resembles a huge board game, where passage from one space to the next takes on symbolic meaning. In the Alchemist's Gardens, the visitor moves through three large squares, from black to white to red, a transition also "from darkness to light, from still waters to the spring of knowledge, from narrow paths to radiance."[71] Every detail of the plan has an ancient symbolic meaning. Marie de Larouzière comments that alchemy quite naturally shares with landscape architecture a fascination for forms, colors, and numbers. Next door is the Botanical Garden of Magic Plants, which pays homage not to esoteric research but to folk wisdom. Here two perpendicular axes—a canal cut in half by a pergola—are surrounded by large squares enclosed with live willow hedging. The tallest plants (small trees) are at each end, with the lowest (aromatic herbs) in the center. All have discreet labels, which provide interesting and amusing information about their origin and uses.

The Noria Gardens are much more closely related to the surrounding landscape, deliberately

set parallel to the house on one side and hills on the other, so that they may serve as foreground for the view from the house. Each feature of the distant panorama connects with a particular axis of the garden: One path leads toward the Mont Aigu, a line of cypresses points toward a hilltown, while an orchard planted in rows frames distant fields. Visitors have their own entrance apart from the house and first find themselves in a grove of pomegranate trees flanking a long pool. The designers consider that the management of sun and shade is both physical and metaphysical, as in Middle Eastern gardens. At the same time, the rill inserted into ocher-toned concrete echoes the work of Mexican architect Luis Barragan, whom these designers much admire. Maurières judges that the Noria Gardens borrow Mediterranean models in their formal elements, in their use of water, and the choice of plants. But this is a Mediterranean without the sea, a world of earth and wind, of farming and irrigation, of fresh running water, of fruit swollen with sugar and sun, and of fragrant flowers. And yet the colored concrete introduces a disconcerting note of modernity, which goes far beyond the clichés of pebble paving, pergolas, and terra-cotta pots.[72]

Maurières and Ossart want a new vocabulary to describe this style: "The term 'symbolic' is too religious, the term 'didactic' is too simplistic, the term 'philosophical' is too pretentious." The Deparis family links their work to eighteenth-century conceptions, more philosophical than religious, suggestive of reverie and contemplation, expressing ideas and telling stories. Whatever terms are used, all of their work is marked by this marriage of intellect and sensuousness, curiosity and playfulness.

Above left:
Ossart and Maurières often use long rills, here in the Botanical Garden of Magic Plants.

Above right and opposite:
Around the pool of the Red Square are 33 solar rays, outlined with "Prestige de Bellegarde" roses, dwarf pomegranates, and climbing roses ("Red parfum").

Notes: [72] *Personal correspondence with Arnaud Maurières.*

A Giant Chessboard

A "Folly" in the Gard

Area: About 5 acres. Creators: Pascal Cribier (with the collaboration of Lionel Guibert), Jean-Michel Wilmotte (architect). Restoration of the house in 1993, garden begun in 1996.

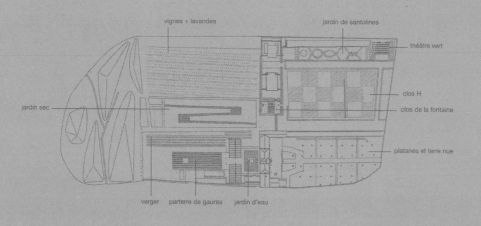

——————— Contemporary art lovers first had this eighteenth-century hunting lodge restored by French architect Jean-Michel Wilmotte. For the creation of a garden in the abandoned park, Wilmotte recommended Pascal Cribier and Lionel Guibert, like himself well known for their modern interpretations of historic sites.

All worked in close collaboration with the owners to create a series of independent spaces, each with its own character, connected by a layout that favors right angles and long perspectives. Hedges of evergreen oaks help define space without the complete enclosure of green rooms. Transitions remain gentle, and exuberant plantings further soften these geometries in a thousand pleasant and unexpected ways, sometimes smothering them entirely, depending on the season. For example, a huge rectangle has been planted with rows of red gaura in a grid of box hedging—two different varieties to contrast two different tones of green. By mid-summer, seen from ground level, the box lines have almost disappeared.

The movement and color of flowers predominates, transforming the gaura into a red sea rippling in the breeze. The grid pattern, so strong earlier and later, is by then discernible only from the windows of the château.

Such inventions abound all over the garden. Often the scenes are simple to the point of minimalism and hidden from view until unveiled to best effect at the last minute. The park includes an embroidered parterre of silver santolina with golden bank plantings; a green theater with fastigate olive trees; the Fountain Close with its bulb collections, lotus, and pergola of Japanese wisteria; a dry garden full of butterflies drawn by a selection of the best plants from the famous Fillipi nurseries; a broad

field alternating vines and lavender planted diagonally with respect to the park's main sight lines; an orchard with its two-toned ballota striping; a privet wood underplanted with a collection of jonquils; a water garden; a secret red garden; and a small fruit and cutting garden labyrinth. The entire sequence has been equipped with subtle night lighting and sound: "You can hear Mozart anywhere in the garden," says the owner proudly. This vast checkerboard is extended beyond the walls by the rows and squares of venerable olive orchards—the traditional patchwork.

The owners have also planned locations for specially commissioned sculptures to be made on site. David Nash spent two weeks at the château before creating portraits of the couple in charred wood: *The King* and *The Queen*. These are intended to preside over the most ambitious garden, still to come, which will tell the story of their lives. Pascal Cribier planned for this space a series of nine interconnecting squares each about nine hundred square feet, to be outlined in wood. Various artists will create sculpture to illustrate important moments from the past. Each enclosure combines different red foliage plants, usually a ground cover and a shrub, to enhance the sculptures. For example, sedem "Red Munstead" should mix with *Dodonea viscosa* "Purpurea" while *Cordyline*

Notes: [73] *Monique Mosser, "Le XXIe siècle sera jardinier," p. 231–241 dans* Le Jardin, notre double: Sagesse et déraison, *Éditions Autrement, collection "Mutations" no 184, March 1999, p. 237.*

australis "Purpurea" goes with red-leafed elderberry, and the small black grass *Ophiopogon japonica* "Nigrescens" with *Pittosporum tenuifolium* "Purpureum." A long straight rill runs through several squares. The presentation is not intended to be chronological, however, as the owner explains: "Time is not linear but circular, and this will be a genuinely metaphysical garden."

In this property, traditional agricultural geometries have been converted into an ambitious work of art, though its grand manner is perhaps more common near Paris than in the south. The designers are also plantsmen, however,

for whom plant growth is the stuff of art. Monique Mosser, a garden historian who often works closely with Pascal Cribier, admires his approach.

For Cribier, a garden does not depend on a great mass of fancy materials or equipment but on "holding" space, in the full sense of the word, thanks to the plants [...] There is a modern style in which the architectural use of plants suffices to create whole new landscapes, variations on scale which are neither natural nor derived from older models.[73]

This observation made about another project also fits these serial gardens by the Rhone.

V stone lines

P rovence can boast magnificent terraced hillsides, steep slopes layered by drystone retaining walls. This special type of sculpted landscape evolved sporadically, according to recent estimates,[75] from Gallo-Roman times through the nineteenth century. Farmers painstakingly removed stones from their land, then recycled them as retaining walls to reduce erosion and facilitate cultivation. Such sites have always needed constant upkeep. Abandoned to sheep, wild boar, or simply encroaching forest, their walls soon crumble into grassy heaps. Water management is essential: Drainage ditches must allow for fast runoff after heavy storms to prevent walls from buckling and collapsing. Rainwater is often stored in cisterns on site, although the crops grown on terraced hillsides—vines, olive trees, chickpeas or buckwheat—were chosen for drought-resistance. In Europe, terraced hillsides are found mainly in Mediterranean regions. No one really knows why. Perhaps it was because farmland is steeper here and the storms more violent.

Stone lines also belong to Europe's great garden heritage. Italian Renaissance estates are steeply terraced, whereas formal French parks near Paris involve graduated levels on land that is almost flat, their original functions now remote. Around 1780, Thomas Blaikie, a Scots gardener promoting the new "English" style, worked for some years in France. He complained (in his own inimitable language) of the "vanity of Le Nôtre of which every French man braggs [...] his plans was noble allthough the reverse of Nature, always those Stiff terrasses and extravagant Staires."[75] Geoffrey Jellicoe, a great twentieth-century landscape architect and historian, remarked that terraces "designed by Le Notre were on a grander scale than those in Italy, but in general, as at St Germain en Laye, they lay along the land rather than being carved from it."[76] Terracing counts again in Riviera designs of

the Belle Époque (notably those of Peto and Forrestier). Here their steep topography is once again Mediterranean. Marie-Laure de Noailles remembers them from her childhood in the 1920s at the Villa Croisset in Grasse: "Drystone terraces like the steps of a giant staircase were meant for sun worship."[77] The hillsides of Grasse in those days were working landscapes where terraced olive trees protected a wealth of flowering plants grown for the perfume industry.

In the great historic gardens where symmetry is valued, walls are as straight and regular as possible. The effect is essentially architectural. In working farmland, stone lines closely follow the natural contours of the land, and as a result, there are neither parallel lines nor two spaces with the same shape or dimensions. An interesting combination appears in the gardens of Serre de la Madone in Menton, begun in 1924. Here Lawrence Johnston, creator of Hidcote Gardens in England, imposed symmetry in the garden's center but played with agricultural irregularity on the edges.[78]

Today, the public is rediscovering this rural heritage, which links gardens and landscape in so many interesting ways. Efforts to preserve sites and ancient skills mix with experimental landscape art such as the "garden in Provence" recently created by the great Scots garden-maker Ian Hamilton Finlay.[79] The region can now boast several *Conservatoires de terrasses* and numerous workshops for training both professionals and vacationers in age-old building skills. Some especially beautiful hillsides have been listed, at Beaumes-de-Venise for example. The owners of such sites now

maintain them proudly, even in suburban housing developments. Retired craftsmen have been known to restore walls along communal byways simply for the love of work well done. In earlier centuries, of course, everyone participated, and any passerby might replace stones fallen during a storm.

Stone terracing creates an unusual alliance between natural landscape and human activity. These lines are built by man and imposed on the site, but they use materials and contours that the land itself provides. In Provençal *bastide* parks, such walls provide a "middle ground" linking the rough rock outside to statues and balustrades carved from the same stone within. All three stages—spontaneous, utilitarian, and ornamental—happily coexist on the same site. The same continuum exists with plants such as box, rosemary, laurel, and viburnum,

species that grow untamed on the hillside but convert easily into functional hedging or sculpted parterres and topiary. The hedge, like the stone wall, may separate garden and landscape spatially, but it also connects them because the same stone and the same plants appear in the wild, in retaining walls and windbreaks, and as pure "art." In this sense, formal and wild gardens in Provence are in fact versions of each other. This is all the more so because the hillside, however untamed its growth may now seem, has been humanized for millennia. This vernacular continuity does not exist in regions where farmland and forest, "culture" and "nature," are experienced as opposites. It does not imply domination, however—far from it. In the Mediterranean, human activity is at best a fragile dialogue with natural forces far too violent to ever imagine subduing.

Terracing challenges other clichés about gardens and landscape. Can one define a "garden" as a walled enclosure and "landscape" as limitless? Stone lines constitute internal divisions and boundaries at the same time! They provide shelter without enclosing. Another problematic opposition is the one between "formal" clarity and "natural" mystery.[80] Terraced landscapes are both formal and mysterious, orderly and secret, geometric to the point of minimalism, while allowing sheltered nooks and crannies for wild fauna and self-sown flora. The formal patterning of their vineyards and orchards is carpeted in spring with "natural" wildflower meadows, rich carpets of spring bulbs. Peter Klasen, a German abstract painter, played on these contrasts by building a resolutely minimalist house on terraces near Grasse next to

an abandoned stone shepherd's hut. Velvet lawn in the heart of the garden is surrounded by seemingly spontaneous meadow and woodland, artfully arranged by designer Camille Muller.[81] Architecture historians often cite Mallet-Stevens's villa at Hyères, which contains the Cubist garden of Gabriel Guevrekian, isolated from its surroundings. Below the villa, usually forgotten, is one of the region's most beautiful layered gardens. Terraces unite architecture, agriculture, and nature with infinite variation. This Mediterranean genre still has much to tell us about human partnership with the land.

Notes: [74] *See Régis Ambroise, Pierre Frapa, Sébastien Giorgis,* Paysages de terrasses *(Edisud, 1989) and Jean-François Blanc,* Terrasses d'Ardèche, paysages et patrimoine *(Le Cheyard, 2001).* [75] *Thomas Blaikie,* Diary of a Scotch Gardener at the French Court at the end of the Eighteenth Century *(Routledge & Sons, 1931), p 192.* [76] *"Terrace, terrace garden" in Geoffrey Jellicoe, Susan Jellicoe, Patrick Goode, Michael Lancaster,* The Oxford Companion to Gardens *(Oxford University Press, 1986), p 552.* [77] *Quoted in Laurence Benaïm,* Marie-Laure de Noailles: La vicomtesse du bizarre *(Grasset, 2001), p 43.* [78] *See Louisa Jones,* Serre de la Madone *(Actes Sud, 2001). Available in English.* [79] *See Ian Hamilton Finlay,* Fleur de l'Air: A Garden in Provence, *edited by Pia Maria Simig (Wild Hawthorn Press, 2004).* [80] *See Russell Page,* Education of a Gardener *(Penguin, 1983), p 94. Page says that the debate about formal and informal gardening is sterile. For his opinion on terraced gardens, see p. 70.* [81] *See Louisa Jones,* L'Esprit nouveau des Jardins: un art un savoir faire en Provence *(Hachette, 1998).*

Opposite, top to bottom: Farm terracing in the Ardèche; Italianate terracing at Serre de la Madone in Menton; contemporary Land Art by Simone Kroll.

Opposite, bottom right: Looking down from terraces imagined by Bruno Leroy for gastronome Lydie Marshall in Nyons.

Above left: A fine mix of England and Provence near Grasse.

Above right: Old and new lines by designer Camille Muller and architect Christophe Petticolo for painter Peter Klasen.

Gentle Minimalism

An Olive Orchard Near Grasse

Area: About 10 acres. Creators: Jacques and Peter Wirtz (landscape architects).
Begun in 1998.

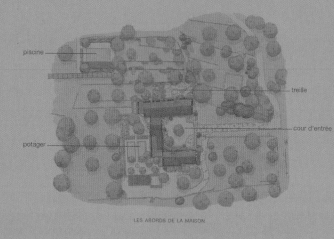

LES ABORDS DE LA MAISON.

———————— Garden writer Catherine Laroze says of the Wirtz
team, father and son, that their gardens bring to life "brute,
rough-hewn forces as vast and silent as steppes; incisive
and willful geometries emerging in dense, shadowy forms."[83]
Sometimes austere, sometimes luxuriating in Flemish fancy,
their works are huge landscape sculptures.

Notes : [83] *Catherine Laroze, Les Jardins de Jacques Wirtz (Fondation pour l'Architecture), p 9.*

On this Riviera hillside, their monumental art has a deceptively traditional appearance. It begins with the carefully shaped, silvery crowns of four hundred olive trees, some over a thousand years old. Between their substantial trunks are broad stretches of dry grass, nothing else. Absence counts here as much as presence, void as much as mass. The trees rise from rhythmic lines of stone walls, low but well-defined. The graphic effect varies with angle of vision, moving from the gate below (east), up to the small parking area behind the house (northwest). The farmhouse, dating from 1641, sits under the crest of the hill, visible from everywhere without being central or dominating. Built from the same stone as the walls, taken from the land itself, it seems wedded to the site, the vital heart from which all lines emerge.

This property had a famous destiny: between 1968 and 1986 it belonged to British film star Dirk Bogarde, who described it at length in his memoirs.[84] Bogarde first loved its abandoned fields—magic carpets of anemones, hyacinths, and violets covering whole terraces, as they still do today. The collapsed walls, remnants of former cultivation, at first seemed romantically wild. Bogarde's Provençal mason made him a list of local fauna and flora to be found on his property, from the fox to the orchids. But then the same man introduced him to a Tunisian apprentice who proved a genius at transforming those picturesque piles of stones into walls. It took him twenty years.

When the current owners arrived, many years later, restoration was needed once again. The Wirtz duo rearranged the terracing more

Above:
Terraced landscapes allow for complex contrasts between open and closed spaces, different from those possible on other sites.

Right:
Olive trees on the Riviera, spared by the frosts that wasted western Provence in 1956, are often living sculptures in their own right. These are beautifully maintained by a certain Monsieur Machiavelli, who once taught pruning at an agricultural college.

Notes: **84** *Dirk Bogarde's autobiographical series includes:* An Orderly Man, Backcloth, and A Short Walk from Harrod's *(all published by Penguin).*

Opposite, left to right
and top to bottom:
Four dogs keep watch on the
four hundred olive trees of the
domain. All the gates are extremely
simple, rustic in appearance but
incorporating modern technology.
The entrance to the potager with
its curtain of lindens. The main
gate with two rams' heads.

Above:
The house rests in the heart of the
hill without dominating it.

Opposite:
One of the designers' main tasks was to simplify transitions like this one leading to a pool created by Dirk Bogarde.

Above, left and right:
Everywhere trees emerge directly from the ground, with nothing planted at their feet, leafy shade trees contrasting with dark cypress candles.

artistically, but still not symmetrically. The general plan is now both closer to its agricultural past and in accord with contemporary minimalism. Certain trees were restored, including some of Bogarde's beloved cypresses, whereas others were removed or transferred to become accents in strategic spots. Tree trunks play an important role in the balance of lines and forms. A row of pleached lindens forms a rectangular curtain, which now hides the entrance to a new, walled vegetable garden. This vertical green architecture, typical of northern formal parks, connects the house to its outdoor dining room. Here as elsewhere the tree trunks are bare right down to ground level, so that their lines stand in clear perpendicular contrast with the ground,

whether they are set in gravel, paving stones, or grass.

Detail has been carefully planned everywhere: stone steps connecting levels are built discreetly into the wall; the modern metallic entrance gate is covered with old wood; the drive up the hill incorporates an elegant but almost invisible drainage system, solid enough to deal with violent southern storms. Everywhere the most modern technology blends with what Jacques Wirtz calls "the wisdom of the ages." Formalism that might seem austere is softened by gentle tones of brown, gray, and green, and by natural textures, rough and subtly sensuous. The only real lawn is the passage between house and pool, particularly soft for bare feet. Climbing

roses and the citrus trees of the potager give off subtle perfumes. This minimalist landscape is also a pleasure garden.

Agriculture here slips into art. The garden melts into its surroundings, its limits appearing blurred even though it is well protected from intruders and has close neighbors. The boundaries farther up are hidden by a grove of oaks that tumble down to the east, accompanied by swaths of wild broom. To the west, along the road that moves to the upper olive terraces, Bogarde had already planted a huge stand of golden bamboo, which, far from shocking in this context, suits the style beautifully by its

very simplicity. From the house, nothing blocks the plunging view toward Grasse on one side and on the other, to the sea. The lower parts of the hillside, built up, are hidden by the crowns of the olive trees. It is easy to believe that there are no neighbors at all.

The current owners wanted above all "to keep things as natural as possible, indoors and out. Few or no flowers in the garden, no pictures or carpets in the house. The beauty of the landscape seen through the windows, an ever-changing scene, is enough." Less is more.

Above, left and right:
The swimming pool below the house looks like a farm cistern. Its shower head emerges from a clump of rosemary like a lotus seed pod.

Opposite:
Traditionally, stone steps linking terraces are parallel to the walls to reserve maximum space for crops. The Wirtz version is less precarious and adds to the rhythms of the design. The grass linking house and pool is the only true lawn, created for the pleasure of walking barefoot.

Hillside Geometries

A Mountain Winery

Area: About 340 acres. Creators: the owners, Benoît Martin-Prevel (designer),
Daniel Gendre (designer), Marc Nucera (Land Artist). Begun in 1998.

From across the valley, the Domaine de la Verrière
looks like a half-fortified village surrounded by woods, vineyards, and olive groves. An entire hamlet, it was cited as
church property already in the eleventh century. Today its
several houses are mainly set along a cobblestone alley that
crosses the hillside about halfway down.

Left:
The entire hamlet at La Verrière is clearly visible from the opposite slope. Once inside the property, you have a panoramic and ever-changing view of mountain scenery. The swimming pool has been kept as discreet as possible.

Opposite left:
"The Lane" links the different parts of the domain, cheerfully decked with tough flowers self-sown in the cracks between stones: red-and-white flowered centranthus (false valerian), green santolina, and wallflowers.

Right:
The admirable linden tree that marks the turn of the terracing on the hillside, a landscape sculpture by Marc Nucera.

This property now belongs to the Rolet family, a young Franco-American couple starting a new life as vintners and producers of oil and honey. Some buildings have been converted into luxury vacation rentals and seminar rooms. Traditional features are everywhere respected but have been put to new uses. For example, the cobblestone alley (called a *calade* in Provençal) no longer functions as a public thoroughfare, crossing the hillside as directly as possible. Its purpose today is to encourage visitors to linger pleasantly along the way. With this in mind, the main entrance gate has been moved up one level so that it opens onto a welcoming courtyard, opposite the medieval window of the caretakers' house. A few steps on each side of a fountain connect this space with the lane below.

The original agricultural terracing has similarly been restored with different aims in mind. Old

materials mask new technology: Blocks of stone quarried on site now hide reinforced concrete retaining walls. New drainage pipes required more than six miles of ditches. The landscape team took charge of these major construction jobs after the project proposed by the original architects was turned down, deemed too suburban for this site. Benoît Martin-Prevel explains: "The Rolets wanted a simple, traditional country style combined with something angular and geometrical." The new terracing, which also displays sixty ancient but newly transplanted olives trees, is more closely linked to the buildings than the old. At the same time, its powerful lines bring together the large volumes of the hamlet more coherently. Horizontals become diagonals on the west flank, where a stone-edged ramp now

descends in a zigzag through the woods to a walled vegetable garden and a new pond at the bottom of the hill. The pivot here is a magnificent linden tree sculpted by Marc Nucera. At La Verrière, his art is present in many places, accompanying and softening the geometric patterning. It also helps integrate existing landscape elements into the new design.

But while the stone lines have become more geometrical, even abstract, the overall spirit remains ecological. "We wanted to unite the powerful stone presence of these old houses with their natural environment," explains Mr. Rolet, who adds:

Erosion, due to violent seasonal storms, had little by little transformed the edges of the property into a kind of wasteland. The new structuring of the terraces gives back a

sense of rootedness to the whole hillside. At the same time, we are sixteen hundred feet above sea level and it often freezes in the winter. The main limitation in planting has been the need for hardy varieties that are also drought-resistant and thrive in full sunshine. The wild vegetation takes over once more as you move away from the heart of the hamlet. In the woods you can find more than a dozen species of wild orchid. We want to lay out botanic trails starting out down by the pond.

Benoît Martin-Prevel considers that "the whole restoration has been planned to encourage walking—it's a whole scenography of space."

Everywhere, pocket gardens have been set into the stone framework, "loosely spilling over with small, tough plants." These touches of color often come from local, self-sowing species such as thymes, rosemaries, borages, dorycniums, Clary sage, hollyhocks and wallflowers. The only small patch of lawn is reserved for children's play, in a closed space near the swimming pool.

The domain also has a beautiful, formal "medieval" garden, a medicinal collection composed of twelve raised square beds enclosed in woven-wicker fencing. Here the designers were able to give full rein to their love of botany, a passion shared by the Rolets. Each bed

Above left:
The new pond at the bottom of the hill near wild woodland where botanic trails will be laid out.

Center:
Marc Nucera makes garden furniture from old plane trees, pieces of a puzzle that could be reassembled in the shape of the original trunk. Thus the memory of the tree lives on.

Right:
The Medieval Medicinal Garden, with its woven-wicker fencing.

represents one part of the body and displays the plants reputed to heal it. In the angles are beds consecrated to the four elements. The one representing Earth has mainly bulbs, Water has a small pool, Sky is planted with blue flowering plants, and Fire with species that "burn," such as nettles.

Benoît Martin-Prevel studied agronomy and urban planning before graduating from the landscape architecture school at Versailles. At La Verrière, he and Xavier Rolet agreed on maintenance that would respect natural process. The owners continue to explore every aspect of their site, not to control it but to enjoy it. They want their gardens to harmonize with their hillside's rich spirit of place for years to come.

Marine Terraces

An Admiral's Perch Near Toulon

Area: Under half an acre, including the house. Creators: the owners, Yves Hervé (designer). Begun in 1998.

———————— Roman architects used the term *villa suburbana* for houses offering country seclusion and pleasures although situated close to the heart of a town. Around 1800, an admiral built such a mansion overlooking the harbor of Toulon. The hillside's first terracing was no doubt built at this time—by convicts. The current owner spent school vacations here and later on was able to buy the property he had loved as a child. Once retired, he wanted to convert its steep slope, inaccessible to heavy machinery, into a series of gardens. Among all the designers he approached, Yves Hervé was the only one willing to take on such a difficult job.

Left:
This steep and inaccessible slope,
overgrown with strong plants that
were breaking down the walls,
appealed to both owners and
designer by its great beauty. It
is now a sumptuous garden.

Right:
Fifteen feet separate the house
terrace from the one below. The
axis established by the double row
of cypresses is an illusion, as is
the apparent symmetry of the
lower level.

Opposite:
The waterlily pool seen from below.
Its grotto is invisible until you are
right in front of it.

Following pages 198-199:
The Florentine parterre seen from
above; steps coming down from
the road, well hidden from the
entrance.

Page 200:
Claude's vegetable garden at the
bottom, where the cypress avenue
ends. "Ox Heart" and "Improved
Saint Pierre" tomatoes are his
favorites.

Page 201:
Hidden treasure is everywhere in
this garden, here behind an
Aeonium arboreum "Zwartkop."

Notes: [85] *A famous botanic garden
near Menton but in Italy: Giardini
Botanici Hanbury, administered by
l'Università degli Studi di Genova,
43, C.so Montecarlo - La Mortola,
18039 Ventimiglia, Italia.
Tel: (+39) 0184-22.98.52
Fax: (+39) 0184-22.92.20
[87] See address list at the back.*

ervé has long been well known for his collection of ornamental sages, and in 1990 he became the first French nurseryman to show at Hampton Court. He also loves digging around flea markets—as does his client, with whom he often goes bargain-hunting. As a result, every object, every stone, every rare plant in this garden has its own story.

The house sits on the edge of the cliff with a plunging view of the sea. The main garden unfolds beside it around a big swimming pool and includes two outdoor dining rooms—one in full sunshine with a view, and one shaded by a giant eucalyptus. The layout is regular, certain shrubs are formally pruned, and there are colorful flowers throughout. From this esplanade you can clearly see the hillside opposite, wooded with cork oaks, Aleppo pines, and date palms, like dark green waves tumbling down the ravine toward the sea. But you cannot see the terraced garden below without leaning over the balustrade.

Fifteen feet below is the second level, where three different gardens are separated by the buttresses of the retaining wall. The south end has a new sculpture-fountain, the middle one a grotto and waterlily pool. To the north is the "Florentine parterre," inspired by the Aromatic Gardens of La Mortola.[86] Viewed from above, its apparent symmetry is an optical illusion adjusted for this angle of vision. Seen on the level, its irregular outlines frame a romantic stone portal (a flea market find), which Hervé has surrounded with an exuberant planting

of white buddleia, myrtles, and a *Viburnum carlesii* with creamy, scented flowers in spring. A pergola made from espaliered lemon trees copies a similar one seen in the gardens at the Chèvre d'Or.[86]

Designer and owners experience this garden as an ongoing game, to be played with patience to make the pleasure last. They recently decided to add a double row of cypresses extending straight down from the house level to the bottom of the hill. It seems to accompany a staircase, but this is another elegant illusion. Lower levels are in fact reached by means of small flights of steps hidden at the ends of terraces, a zigzag descent which unveils different cross perspectives at each lap. The lowest level is the vegetable garden, lovingly tended by the gardener and friend Claude, who sets out little fennel plants accompanied by his favorite robin. Each of the narrow levels is dominated by high stone walls, and therefore planted with varieties that can both climb and spill over. Everything remains intimate; some details are designed for close-up viewing, while others forge links between levels or frame long perspectives. Many outer edges have simple iron railings that allow you to see beyond but some have, on the contrary, a narrow hedge that encloses you in a secret garden. Constant pruning is needed to keep everything fluid and indeed to make passage even possible.

To restore certain walls, the owners bought up old stones from a cemetery, put up for sale by a marble mason. Claude considers; "It's beautiful for a tombstone to end up in a garden!" As for the plants, Hervé has an unparalleled network of nurserymen friends. The lemon trees for the pergola were pruned for three years in the Dordogne before arriving here. The box plants come from Jacques Seghers near Paris. The sages, especially a curtain of *Salvia guaranatica* that intertwines with olive trees in summer, are from his own nursery. The garden overflows with botanic and horticultural treasures—hundreds of bulbs, many saved from old gardens sacrificed to developers. Flowers perfume the air season by season. Hervé considers that he began his career designing gardens around plants, but now makes "far more structured gardens, where mineral elements are strongest." This garden illustrates a harmonious and much-loved balance between the two.

Picturesque Formalism

Woodland Walls in the Luberon

Area: 7.5 acres. Creator: Michel Semini (designer).
House built in 1975, restored in 1991; garden begun in 2000.

_____ The Luberon hills often appeal to cosmopolitans, who prefer country quiet to the sophisticated and overbuilt Riviera. Living here also seems more relaxed than in the Alpilles farther south. Designer Michel Semini explains the differences: "In the Luberon, spectacular views are much more common. Gardens are more open but also more rustic. In the Alpilles the mistral wind is felt much more; gardens are walled in, protected by cypress hedging, more private and often more formal."[87]

Notes: [87] _Michel Semini and Hugues Bosc,_ De Pierre et de Nature _(private publication, 2003)._

Left and opposite:
The entire hillside was reshaped
to set off the finest oaks of this
wild woodland. The stone walls,
sometimes restored, sometimes
new, impose curves as much as
they follow existing contours,
carefully avoiding the straight
lines of the smaller gardens. Local
limestone ages fast and cemented
joints are kept very discreet.

Following pages, left:
The path up to the pool, northwest,
unveils a series of intimate scenes.

Right:
Here a row of *Ceratostigma
plumabo* underscores a wall, but
leaves the grass bare for a display
of moving shadows.

Semini's design here differs completely from his work for Pierre Bergé in the Alpilles (p. 52). This site was long abandoned to oak and pine woods, without losing its panoramic views. Its hilly terrain with long perspectives, the massive presence of rock and stone, natural springs at almost every level, and an impressive number of enormous old trees cannot but evoke the Picturesque mode once again.

Semini chose to mix genres however, combining soft curves with right angles, setting off giant tree trunks with intimate plant mosaics and tapestries. The usual opposition between formal geometries and natural curves does not apply here at all, neither in the layout nor in the plantings. Variations in scale and in plant configurations create a carefully balanced harmony within this natural landscape, a typical "*colline*" or lightly wooded hillside of Provence.

The house, recently built, then restored with interiors by designer France Loeb, sits partway up the slope. It is solidly constructed with the same local stone used for the sustaining walls

Opposite and above:
Near the pool, the meandering path ends with large-scale formal patterning. These twelve vast rectangles of evergreen honeysuckle (*Lonicera nitida*) lend themselves to graphic games of light and shade, while maintaining a suitably simple foreground for the view beyond.

Following pages, left:
The house lies on three levels, each opening onto the hillside. Here box globes mix with heavenly bamboo, abelias, vinca, pittosporum, and eleagnus. Against the wall, a young oak with gnarled trunk is a sculpture.

Right:
The elegant formal pool below echoes the right angles of the swimming pool at the top. Water for these grand stretches of lawn comes by pipeline from the Durance river.

that extend its lines. It is not the house one sees first, however, but the trees, very much the stars of the show. Dozens of white and holm oaks were removed so that the best would thrive. The entire terrain was restructured to set them off to advantage. Semini made no plan on paper, however; he preferred to walk round and mark the changes he wanted with biodegradable spray paint directly on the contours of the land. The newly built retaining walls look as if they have always been there, for this limestone quickly takes on a patina.

Semini experimented with the terracing in daring ways. Russell Page, an influential British designer of an earlier generation, judged that there must always be a broad, flat space around a house set on a steep slope. Otherwise, it may seem precariously perched, about to tumble down the hill. Here the paved area extending outdoors from the main living room is not wide, but it seems well-anchored thanks to a fine old oak tree, rooted far below, which was allowed to grow up right through it! The crown of this tree now shades the house while its branches frame a spectacular view of the village. Seen from the entrance below, the house does look perched, but from above, it seems rather to nestle—like the medieval hilltown across the valley.

Page also notes that, in gardens on steep hillsides, people rarely visit the parts far from the house. Here too Semini has an unusual

solution: The arrival gate is at the lowest point, the road from there up to the house gently graded to allow time to admire the elegant buttressing, formal pool, and plantings of the lowest levels. The swimming pool is at the top of the hill, and some of the most interesting secret gardens line the path that leads up to it. Gate and pool are, of course, visited daily.

The small gardens by the house are all simple compositions, different on each level, each with its pattern of globes, squares, fountains, and sculpted trees. Evergreen and evergray foliage predominate: box, rosemary, various pittosporums, *Eleagnus ebbingei*, euonymus, photinia, ceanothus. Once at the top, above most of the trees, the scale changes completely: Twelve vast rectangles of lonicera create a minimalist parterre as foreground for the generous view. On the very summit of the hill is a simple field of lavender. On the other side of the house, contours are broader and softer. An olive orchard spreads between outcroppings of rough stone and a shelter belt of trees on the edge of the property. But it is still from the entrance gate that one has the best perspective on the piled-up levels and lines that make this garden so striking. Some of the terraces are like draperies, their plantings like embroidered hems. The Luberon style may be rustic and is sometimes quite rough, but this garden is highly refined.

Sculpture and Horticulture

A Photographer's Holiday Home

Area: 4.5 acres. Creators: the owner, Anthony Paul (designer).
Begun in 1998.

———————————— Tony M., a photographer who founded his
own agency, collects contemporary art. Anthony Paul, a
well-known British garden designer, also directs a photo
agency. Anthony and his wife, Hannah Peschar, run an
outdoor sculpture gallery in Sussex.

All this talent conspired to transform a modest farmhouse in Provence into an elegant and engaging work of art. Tony has been exploring the back roads of the region for years on holidays and preferred, for his retirement, the area northeast of Avignon. He feels that the fashionable areas farther south, in the Luberon and the Alpilles, are already too crowded with foreigners. He bought this place because of its dramatic outlook on the famous Mont Ventoux. When working on both house and garden, he used his photographer's eye to frame views and unveil the panorama in several stages. Visitors entering the property first glimpse the mountain through the gate, beyond a courtyard, and through an arch. Tony and Anthony Paul, his designer, both imagined the layout as a series of "events," an approach Tony much admires in Japanese gardens. A complete walk around is needed to appreciate fully all angles and perspectives.

The house stands on a low but steep hill, overlooking, on the view side, a patchwork of fields below the silver-tipped cone of the mountain. Low stone terracing accompanies a narrow path leading down one side of the slope and up the other. The central spaces are planted with diagonal rows of lavender (*Lavendula "Grosso"*), which creates very contemporary patterning. A checkerboard of various fruit trees at the base of the hill connects the garden to the plain beyond, linking new landscape geometries to age-old field patterns. Each of the sculptures, mainly from Hannah's gallery, is placed to set off a particular perspective on the countryside.

Near the house, other stone walls in brilliant white limestone become sculptures in their own right. Their function is not to enclose, nor even to hold up the slope. but simply to lead off in fluid lines towards the landscape. In one place, two sections do not quite meet, creating a

Above left:
The south-facing courtyard has a mixed planting of pittosporums, abelias, shrubby sages, star jasmine, *Dorycnium hirsutum*, and buddleias. Each transition is planned to frame a faraway view or a nearby sculpture, or both at the same time.

Right:
A bench designed by Anthony Paul sets off the sculpture, *New Lovers*, by Marzia Colonna.

Above left:
The only lawn of the domain, intended for grandchildren, under a brand-new linden tree in the southern courtyard.

Right:
Water from the fountain of the Country Curate's garden cascades into an old stone feeding trough. The owner calls this a "sculpture-event."

Notes: **88** *See this artist's website http://chrisbooth.co.nz.*

gap—another frame—near a pebble fountain. Elsewhere there is a tower reminiscent of the old stone shepherd huts found in various parts of Provence, but slimmer and taller. Tony much admires Andy Goldsworthy's walls and cairns, as well as the landscape sculptures of New Zealand artist Chris Booth.[88] But if the inspiration is global, the techniques are local: Anthony Paul, who comes from New Zealand himself, called in local masons and feels that he learned a lot from their work. The results apparently please the rural neighbors: One rebuilt a wall of his own imitating the slightly wavy contour of Paul's design.

Tony and his team of outsiders have been well received in the community, thanks to contacts provided by generous and helpful neighbors. Many specialists were needed—the pool experts came from England—but Anthony Paul's local correspondent has been Bruno Collado, a

gardener-designer in his own right. Bruno appreciates the design vocabulary used here: traditional elements combined in a modern, cosmopolitan idiom. The diagonals used for the lavender planting and for some paths and walls create a dynamic energy flow. Anthony Paul likes to plant in great swaths, mixing bands of cistus, phlomis and grasses. On the west side of the house, for example, is a walled courtyard called the "country curate's garden." The guest rooms overlook this semiformal parterre, which is regular but unpredictable, flowing and gently geometric. The layout is further softened by a profusion of plants chosen among freeform and "wild"-looking varieties. Many species are originally Mediterranean but are present here in horticultural selections developed in northern Europe: thyme, phlomis, perovskias, teucriums, oreganos, sages, rosemary, cistus, euphorbias, and lavenders among them. Paul adds vibrant

yellow and orange notes to his purples and blues, whether it is with rustic plants like wallflowers and phlomis or exotics from New Zealand. The slope below the pool also mixes northern and local elements: its patch of annual flowers among the fruit trees is a multicolored miniature meadow, contrived here to resemble the floral displays which often occur spontaneously in Provence in the spring.

All these details have but one aim: to link the house to the panorama that surrounds it, nearly full circle. Tony M., always the photographer, notes with a certain humor that some of his views would look good on a calendar. But as a gardener, he also appreciates the variety of this ever-changing show. He is quite in love with "his" mountain, and his camera clicks in all weathers. And although his garden takes flight toward far horizons, it is kept rooted to the spot by its lines of stone and the sculptures, those imported and those built on site. All contribute their solid, mineral, and long-lasting presence.

Community sharing

The landscapes of Provence are well known, but its gardens have long been very private. Today, the recognition of garden-making as a fine art is encouraging owners both to improve their gardens and to open them up to public view. Often art—a temporary exhibition or permanent display—is the very point of opening up a private property. Cultural analyst Anne Cauquelin examines at some length the current convergence in France between gardening and the plastic arts.[90] She observes that contemporary artists work more and more with "the vegetal, with live material." She adds: "Note that I say 'with' and not 'on'![90]

Partnership is the key here, just as in ecological gardening. In fact, Cauquelin's definition of an art installation could apply to anyone's home garden: "an arrangement of objects and individuals in space in such a manner as to make things happen." Many artists working outdoors go further and include the site itself as subject. So it is at Cézanne's studio in Aix-en-Provence, where works created by young artists in the adjacent woodland are temporary, festive, and educational. Similar installations are now commonly found at plant fairs all over the region.

Historic gardens strike another note: They embody site memory while encouraging visitors to acknowledge, appreciate, and help preserve a cultural heritage. The Riviera first began the fashion for historic revivals in the south, especially in the city of Menton. Several active garden clubs and associations now advise members who want to open up old family gardens. Others offer prizes for the restoration of parks, as for other endangered works of art. The government conservancy agency, the Conservatoire du littoral, has saved many fine old coastal properties by direct purchase. It steers a difficult course between conservation and creation, not only in its most famous sites, the Domaine du Rayol near Saint-Tropez or Serre de la Madone in

Menton, but also in lesser-known properties such as the Courbebaisse park in the town of Le Pradet, a property once belonging to an admiral. The Conservatoire's list of its properties in Provence offers many fine examples of landscape gardens and gardened landscapes. Site memory is also the main focus for landscape renovation around famous historic monuments like the Roman aqueduct at the Pont du Gard. Here an imaginative team set aside a piece of the natural setting to illustrate local land use from Roman times. This "garden" is called Mémoire de garrigue.

The boundary separating public from private (like that between garden and landscape) has become more and more permeable. The resulting ventures are often intended to benefit both local communities and visitors from afar. Such are the controversial roundabouts or traffic circles now found at the entrance and exit of even the smallest communities, miniature landscape gardens portraying what each locality deems most essential to its self-image. They show amazing variety. Another

very rich vein is the nursery garden. This is not usually, as might be supposed, a commercial showcase, but a family garden which has proven so engrossing that the owners begin reproducing and sharing their favorite plants. The nursery helps finance the passion, but the latter came first. Yet another genre includes gardens made for a particular public and only rarely opened to the general visitor. Such is the intriguing design conceived for the Institute of the Blind in Marseille (created by Alain Richert and Catherine Willis), Natacha Guillaumont's imaginative design for the homeless in the same city, or the various networks of gardens intended to help the long-term unemployed.[91]

The picture is not all rosy, however. Many town administrations seriously neglect fine gardens on their territory, such as the Fernand Braudel Park created by Alain Farragou at

Seyne-sur-Mer near Toulon, or the fascinating botanical gardens created by the hermit Elie Alexis at La Roquebrussanne east of Aix (restored and maintained by a fervent team of volunteers). Other more enlightened municipalities, like Graveson (p. 232), are now caught up in the national enthusiasm for "green tourism."

The evolution of this movement in Provence has had its ups and downs, or perhaps downs and ups. It is thought-provoking today to reread the comments of Provençal writer Jean Giono, written in 1960.[92] He rails against corrupt administrative manipulations in small towns where promoters exerted undue influence after World War II. Giono proposed tourism as a guarantee of regional authenticity! American writer Susan Sontag argued in the 1970s that modern tourists descend directly from those eighteenth-century connoisseurs who, steeped in the Picturesque vision, perceived landscapes as a sequence of beautiful pictures. The arrival of cheap cameras was just then encouraging the fad for souvenir snapshots. Sontag complained that cameras kept travelers at a distance from the countries they visited, because they experienced them as spectacle, interesting only if photogenic.[93] Those were years when many people in Provence feared to see their countryside reduced to postcard material. A concerned landscape architect, Bernard Lassus, designed a motorway rest area between Nîmes and Arles to make connections both with surrounding landscapes and local history, rather than isolating travelers from the passing show.[94] Can it be said that a whole generation's efforts to avoid this corrosion of cultural values have borne fruit? Experiments like those described below illustrate a balance, successful though often precarious, between local communities and tourism, in which shared gardens and landscapes are the major focus.

Many gardens today are created directly for the public. The great model for the entire southeast remains the Bambouseraie of Prafrance. Despite its remote location, it welcomes as many visitors as the Loire valley château at Villandry—roughly 350,000 annually. The year 2006 marks its 150th birthday. Its rich history and collections are now further enhanced by contemporary land art, the new Dragon Valley created by Eric Borja.[95]

All over France today, the public often views gardens as outdoor cultural venues rather than as places to learn about plants. Their appeal is meant to be both artistic and educational. Visitors do not come so much to "steal" ideas for their own gardens as to enjoy nature

while improving their knowledge. Promotional materials frequently stress a garden's attractions for children because of this educational potential, but also because adults, during the visit, may hope to recover the pleasures and fresh vision of childhood. For all ages, the visit requires active participation in discovery. This goal, often realized, implies an ideal of community sharing.

Opposite, left to right:
Inventive signposting at the "Mémoire de garrigue" site near the Roman Pont du Gard; the cactus gardens of Elie Alexis restored by volunteers; gardens for the homeless at the Abbé Pierre foundation in Marseille, created by Natasha Guillaumont.

Above:
The Bambouseraie of Prafrance, a model for green tourism.

Notes: [89] *See the following: Anne Cauquelin,* Petit traité du jardin ordinaire *(éditions Payot et Rivages, 2003);* L'invention du paysage *(Quadrige PUF, 2000);* Le site et le paysage *(Quadrige PUF, 2002) and* Petit traité d'art contemporain *(Seuil, 1996).* [90] *Cauquelin,* Petit traité du jardin ordinaire, *p 128. The author does, however, point out a number of differences between gardens and installations.* [91] *For all these examples, see address list at the back.* [92] *Jean Giono,* Apprendre à voir, *article dates 13 July 1962.* [93] *Susan Sontag,* On Photography *(Delta, 1977).* [94] *Rest area at Nîmes-Caissargues on the A55 autoroute between Nîmes and the airport Nîmes-Garons, accessible from both directions.* [95] *See Louisa Jones in collaboration with Yves Crouzet,* La Bambouseraie *(Actes Sud, 2004).*

Mandarin's Delight

A Bamboo Nursery Near Grasse

Area: 5 acres. Creator: Benoît Beraud (nurseryman). Begun in 1989.

———— Garden historian John Dixon Hunt suggests that the Picturesque movement in France evolved on the one hand toward exotic scenes (often of Chinese inspiration), and on the other toward sentimental depictions of nature with a moral lesson.[96] Mandarin's Delight combines both visions. At the same time, this garden successfully blends a collection of rare bamboos with wild Provençal woodland.

Notes : [96] *John Dixon Hunt*, The Picturesque Garden in Europe (*Thames & Hudson, 2003*).

Benoît Beraud, its creator, settled here in the Var region in the late 1980s. He recalls, "I came down from Paris to hike. By pure chance I happened on this piece of land—it was fate, but it was also a challenge!" In 1988, he got permission from the local agricultural board to grow bamboo on this site, thus obtaining subsidies to buy the land. In 1989, he planted the collection and began reproduction, and in 1992 he opened the nursery. Today, this small business and the entrance fees to the garden allow Beraud and his family to live here year round.

Long abandoned, the land was already covered with rough woods mixing holm oaks, alder, box, rhamnus, laurel, honeysuckle, and other local species. Should the intrusion of bamboos into this natural vegetation be regarded as shocking? William Robinson,

author of *The Wild Garden* (1870), is often cited as a pioneer by native plant purists. Robinson recommended the planting of bamboos "by quiet Grass walks, in sheltered dells, in the shrubbery, or in little glades in woods"—exactly as is done at Mandarin's Delight. "Their beauty," insisted the English horticulturalist, "is the more precious from their being wholly distinct in habit from any other plants and shrubs that we grow."[97] Benoît only grows those that thrive in Provence, but these number more than eighty varieties.

Visitors arriving at Mandarin's Delight first discover a horseshoe-shaped road, along which are gradually unveiled a series of miniature scenes that Benoît calls his "pocket gardens." Benoît likes to play with unusual objects—Thai statues, low jars, even an old-fashioned baby carriage. Stone heads from Indonesia alternate

Notes : [97] *William Robinson,* The Wild Garden *(Century Publishing, 1983), p.158.*

Above, left to right:
A selection of woodland scenes: Indonesian stone heads; an old well; ruins of the sixteenth-century mill; a bamboo gate; a selection of the eighty bamboo varieties; exotic poultry.

Following pages, left:
Inside the "Cathedral," where the path meanders back and forth over irrigation ditches, allowing close inspection of the bamboo stalks.

Right:
A curtain of bamboos on two levels—*Phyllostachus aurea* behind a hedge of *Sasa vitchi*, two-toned in winter. Béraud points out that bamboo hedging, unlike cypress or laurel, needs pruning only once a year.

with tortuous tree trunks. He also experiments with different levels of vegetation, from the mossy ground up to the crown of an ornamental cherry. Self-sown laurels wind themselves among the golden stalks of certain bamboos, while a silvery eleagnus has been pruned to surround another grouping (sea-green this time). His painter's eye has organized subtle mixtures, never forced. They can be admired in rain as well as in sunshine—one of the great advantages of bamboo. Benoît points out that some types of foliage absorb light (such as cypresses) and others reflect it (bamboos). He mixes both for varied effects.

The larger landscape garden is approached by a broad path, which first leads downhill to the river Siagne before curving round to return uphill through the woods. Another series of sometimes unexpected scenes unfolds along this road, making the most of sun and dappled shade through intermingling foliage, punctuated by various objects in wood, stone, or bamboo, all worn by the passage of time. Water is everywhere: springs, streams, old irrigation canals. Ruins reminiscent of the Picturesque genre include both genuine vestiges of a sixteenth-century mill and mock remnants (a Corinthian column on the summit of the cliff). The result, playful and highly enjoyable, might well be the garden Rousseau admires in his novel *La nouvelle Héloïse*: "Everything is verdant, fresh, vigorous, and the gardener's hand is not to be seen. . . . The sinuous paths twist and turn in feigned irregularity, artfully arranged to make the walk last longer."[99]

At the bottom of the valley is an open space with a park for donkeys and ample room for musical or craft events. Sometimes on Sunday,

Left:
The woodland walk at the bottom
of the hill reveals the successful
integration of many different bamboos into the natural Provençal
landscape. At the turn of a path is
a pool, at the foot of the cascade
tumbling down from the old mill.

Opposite:
Thanks to a spring that flows
summer and winter, averaging
8,000 to 9,000 gallons of water
an hour, the Berauds were able to
create their nursery. The resur-
gence is dramatically enhanced
with tree ferns from Tasmania.

the notes of a Japanese woodland pan (the *shakuhachi* flute) can be heard floating above the stands of bamboo. Schoolchildren often come for outdoor classes here, to listen to folktales or learn about the park's fauna. Sometimes these too are exotic. A peacock now inhabits these woods, and when he perches on a treetop to escape the foxes, it is his cry that scares off wild boar.

"Overall," says Benoît, "people leave our place feeling serene and relaxed." This is indeed the atmosphere sought by Chinese mandarins, for whom "a garden must preserve mystery in its passages, its shadows and reflections, be enclosed in its surroundings like a jewel in its case."[99] The Mandarin's Delight with its collection of bamboos fits snugly into its landscape, but at the same time it conjures up other centuries, other continents.

Notes : [98]*Jean-Jacques Rousseau,* Julie, ou, la nouvelle Héloïse, *transl. by Philip Stewart and Jean Vaché, University Press of New England, 1997, p. 393–394.* [99] Les Paradis naturels: Jardins chinois en prose, *collection of texts translated and presented by Martine Vallette-Hémery (Éditions Philippe Picquier, 2001), p. 13.*

A Town for Tomorrow

Graveson, Village in the Alpilles

Areas: The Aquatic Gardens: 4 acres (two more in the works); the Four Seasons Garden: 5 acres. Creators: For the Aquatic Gardens "Aux fleurs de l'eau" (privately owned): Alain Stroppiana; The Garden of the Four Seasons (municipal): David Tresmontant of the Forest Services and Jean-Louis Bayol, of the town council; The Herb Parterre (privately owned): Nelly Grosjean of Vie'Arôme; the collection of 150 fig varieties at the Mas de Luquet (privately owned): Francis and Jacqueline Honoré. Garden specialist at the Graveson Tourist Office: Claire Villero. The Aquatic Gardens were begun in 1987; the Four Seasons Garden in 1999.

———— Graveson is a village of some 3,200 inhabitants, situated between Avignon and Arles. It has everything a Provençal community could wish for: prehistoric, Roman, and medieval vestiges; country craftsmen making créches, harnesses, and church candles; folk festivals including Provençal Christmas, the running of the bulls and the floral parade of Saint-Éloi; an agricultural cooperative dating from 1928; and even its very own belle-époque landscape painter, Auguste Chabaud.

Today, with farming incomes falling off, this town has converted to green tourism. This decision is neither cynical nor nostalgic: The townspeople want tourists but also feel that reviving their local heritage will enrich their own lives. For example, the farmers' market traditionally held on mornings now takes place on Friday evenings for the convenience of working townspeople. The local choir has chosen as its name Un païs pèr deman (a town for tomorrow). The language is old Provençal, but the spirit is entirely forward-looking.

The territory of Graveson includes a large sector of the nearby Montagnette, ten thousand acres of hilly, fragrant pinewood, which this town shares with the neighboring communities of Barbentane, Boulbon, and Tarascon. Three hundred thousand visitors wander here yearly, some to visit a famous monastery (Saint Michel de Frigolet), others to collect fragrant herbs or to bird-watch (rare species are protected here). A major highway and rail line used to cut off the town center from its woodlands, but the municipality has now built an underground pedestrian passageway and laid out hikers' trails. Graveson is once again united with its mountain. Christmas Eve pilgrimages on foot to the monastery have been resumed, and not just for tourists.

Landscape revival is here linked to gardens. Instead of building a football stadium on a vacant lot at the edge of town, the town council opted for a public park, the Garden of the Four Seasons. Hiking trails begin here, there is outdoor theater in summer, and the Magali wine cooperative

Above left to right:
The spectacular water garden imagined, created, and maintained by Alain Stroppiana is the main attraction of the garden community of Graveson—all the pools except those with the giant carp are filled with plants; *Hibiscus coccineus, Ipomoea x imperialis* (blue) and *Ipomoea quamoclit* (red); a mix of perennials with a purple-leafed amaranthus; a happy carp in its pool.

Following pages, left:
Alain Stroppiana, still beginning
as a botanist, knows how to
impose order without constraint,
creating a sense of harmony that
many more experienced gardeners
might envy.

From left to right
and top to bottom:
Hibiscus trionum with *Duranta
repens*; lotus (*Nelumbo nucifera*);
one of Stroppiana's many varieties
of waterlily; *Datura inoxia*.

and a new crafts center are right next door. David Tresmontant of the Forest Services has organized the planting of 2,500 flowering trees and shrubs (107 varieties) and hopes that a national collection of viburnums will be possible. The municipal budget only pays for fifty days a year of upkeep; but the park is popular.

Certain individuals had already started interesting gardens. The aromatherapy center, Vie'Arôme, took over the winery once belonging to the local monastery and planted an educational herb parterre. At the Mas de Luquet, the Honoré family grows 150 varieties of fig and welcomes visitors as well as buyers. But the most famous garden of Graveson, written up by magazines as far away as Japan and Australia, was made by a former builder specializing in

earthworks, Alain Stroppiana. When farming declined, so did his business. In his spare time, he used his bulldozers to create a giant rockery in his family's backyard. Famous specialists helped with the plantings, above all Pierre and Pia Braun (whose nursery of flowering plants is justly renowned). The conception was Stroppiana's, however: "I love spaces that are intimate and yet very open," he explains. Stroppiana's boulders have been assembled to look natural around grottoes and cascades. A series of pools sets off plants, stonework, and his giant carp. This might again be pure Picturesque, were it not for the brilliant light and luxuriant colors. The builder, an expert in his craft, paid careful attention to details such as surfacing for his paths. Instead of cement or

asphalt, he chose a fine gravel called "tapissette," the same used for *boules* and *pétanque* courts in Provence: "It is stable, does not fly around in the wind. Rain damps down the dust and makes the path even firmer. It's a regional material; the color is easy on the eye and gets darker as it ages." His rocks also come from local quarries: Graveson, Tavel, Beaucaire, Les Baux. The water comes from springs on his property, situated on the former bed of the Durance river.

Stroppiana loves his plants, and they seem to love him. He associates whatever appeals to him: rosemary and rhododendrons, cotoneasters and phormiums, weeping birch and creeping grevilleas. He has a good eye, and if his mixtures are sometimes unconventional, they are always harmonious. The visit is refreshing in every respect.

The town council asked Stroppiana to open his garden. He now enjoys his visitors and listens to their comments, whether they be mothers with children, retired people who spend hours here, or passing Australians. He manages the upkeep himself, with family help for selling tickets. In 2005 they had 2,600 visitors.

The village of Graveson now publishes a lush tourist office brochure where it boasts of its "Extraordinary Gardens." The mayor got re-elected, an event that helped ensure continuity. Jean-Louis Bayol, town councilor, feels their efforts have been well received: "People here, mainly of country stock, know the importance of planting for future generations." The example of Graveson may well become a model for other communities.

Opposite:
This garden is also an arboretum: *Eucalyptus gunnii* and *Gingko biloba* stand on the upper slope.

Above:
This park contains other miniature landscapes: here a dry garden, elsewhere a lavender field, a tiny vineyard, an olive orchard, and a rockery using the red stone of Les Baux.

A Painter's Vision Renewed

Botanical Collections in the Var

Area: 20 acres. Creators: Pierre and Henriette Deval (owners 1925–1993)
and their daughter Françoise Darlington-Deval; Bernard Chanut and recently,
Marcus Campbell (gardeners); Pierre Quillier (horticultural advisor).
Restoration begun in 1993.

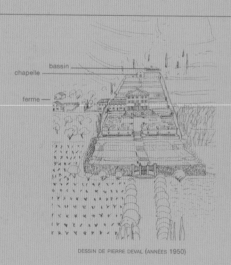

chapelle — bassin
ferme —

DESSIN DE PIERRE DEVAL (ANNÉES 1950)

The restoration of historic properties often means new beginnings. What resources are available in Provence today for an owner who wants to breathe new life into a valuable private garden, protecting her heritage but also sharing it with a wider community? The Domaine d'Orvès is an exceptional property, besieged by vigorous urban expansion, no doubt necessary but not always well planned.

When intimist painter Pierre Deval and his wife bought the property in 1925, the town of La Valette du Var was a market gardener's village particularly blessed by climate and location. Sheltered from the wind by Mount Coudon, watered by well-stocked springs, it specialized then in the production of violets and strawberries.[100] The domaine, situated on the slopes of the Coudon, looked down on the steeple of this charming community. Its own abundant water-flow was directed by two norias through a system of canals (called *goulottes*) for the irrigation of watercress and artichoke plantations, leeks, and even arum lilies. The hillside behind, much

dryer, was covered with olive and almond orchards and vineyards. And then, beginning in 1985, various road projects and housing developments started to encroach on the domain. The painter and his wife began to fight back, and in 1993 managed to get the property listed by the Monuments historiques.

Orvès (also called the Castle of Castellane) has a particularly rich history. This seventeenth-century *bastide* first belonged to the Martini d'Orvès family. Later owners included a series of navy officers who collected exotic plants, some of which still remain. After 1925, the Devals transformed its terraces into such a luxuriant and vital garden that their friend, the

Above left:
Now that distant views are blocked by cypress hedging, the domain has become an enchanting, self-contained world apart. In the foreground, a rare shrub for warm climates: *Cocculus laurifolius*.

Right:
Behind the house, the path leads through local arbutus and laurel hedging. This secret corner is full of spring bulbs—Peruvian scillas and *Tulipa clusiana* among others.

Opposite:
The main axis linking gate and house, edged with very old oleanders, is seen here from the house.

famous Provençal novelist Henri Bosco, congratulated them in these terms: "You have preserved, consolidated, enriched, ornamented and painted a patch of earth that can only be called divine."

Since 1993, Françoise Darlington-Deval has been continuing and enriching the work of her parents. She inherited a property fallen into romantic disrepair and first had to restore the ochre *bastide* with its green shutters, then the pergola and esplanade overlooking two symmetrical long, deep pools. The main approach is a wonderful avenue of very old oleanders with twisted trunks, often painted by Deval. There is also a little chapel, a threshing circle, and remnants of a mine where lime was once excavated. In a farmhouse nearby on the property, Madame Darlington houses young apprentice gardeners from other countries to study Mediterranean plants. She grew up in this place and knows its every scent and murmur. Her childhood still lives on through her father's many drawings and paintings, and it gives her pleasure to share this happy heritage.

Madame Darlington lived for some years in England. Her familiarity with British horticultural networks has helped her create rare plant collections on this site while embellishing the gardens. Luckily she has been blessed with exceptional gardeners and the precious support of a great Mediterranean plantsman, Pierre Quillier, garden curator for the nearby city of Hyères. In recent years, the gardens of Orvès have become a dense, colorful, luxuriant jungle

Page 244:
Madame Darlington and her team work mainly on listed areas near the house, but the hillside behind also shelters many treasures. Red foliage here belongs to a wild *Cotinus coggygria*, commonplace, perhaps, but tough and beautiful.

Page 245 top to bottom and left to right:
Cordylines and agaves in the wood; pools and walls draped with coronillas; *Grevillea juniperina* in the spring; *Ceanothus ceoruleus* "Concha" with its bright blue flowers.

Above left to right:
The layered pools that give such
character to the property, near the
venerable oleanders; a parterre of
Myrsine africana, from which
emerge, each in its season, tulips
and lavender; the chapel with its
old cypresses and laurel hedging.

Page 248:
Terracing formerly used by market
gardeners, still just barely maintained, has great charm. Olive
trees, echiums, rosemary, and
cypress intermingle here.

Page 249:
The swimming pool is completely
surrounded and opens only onto
the sky.

in which each section has its own specialty.
These include acacias, mahonias, hibiscus,
arbutus (*A. glandulosa, A. andrachne*), and tree
ferns. The outer edges of the domain have kept
their traditional vegetation—woodland and
orchard, though the latter now have anenome
carpets in spring. Four new levels between the
bastide and the road display diagonal pools
surrounded by lemon and quince trees, and
lozenge-shaped parterres of rosemary and
pomegranate. There is a new pond to house a
collection of aquatic plants.

Articles in British and Dutch magazines, visits
by specialized international groups, and active
participation in national Garden Open days
have all helped Françoise Darlington-Deval gain
some measure of recognition. She was recently

granted the "Remarkable Garden" label by the
Minister of Culture. The nearby city of Toulon
has no Botanic garden—perhaps Orvès could
supply this need? Finding and filling a unique
niche would certainly help ensure the garden's
future. This story is only just beginning…

Notes : [100] *For the life of this Domain and its owners, see the beautiful
book by Michèle Gorenc,* Deval: Maître d'Orvès *(Editions Autres
Temps, 1997). For more horticultural information, see the article by
Lucy Gent "The Garden at Orvès," in* The Mediterranean Garden
*(journal of the Mediterranean Garden Society, see address list), n° 31,
January 2003.*

Allotment Gardening

The "Castellas" in Marseille

Area: 35 acres, of which half are cultivated; 238 gardens of about 2,000 square feet each, distributed among 9 sections. Creators: Generations of gardeners; current president Gilbert Gelly and secretary Rémy Spehner. First allotments in Marseille in 1905, at the "Castellas" in 1941, open for public visits on special days as of 2002.

_____ "A working-class allotment", writes ethnologist Françoise Dubost, "is neither a private refuge nor yet a public place but something in between. It thrives on neighborly exchanges and mutual support."[101]

Notes : [101] *Françoise Dubost, Les Jardins ordinaires (L'Harmattan, 1997), p. 5.*

The French allotment movement began in 1896 in the north, where a certain Abbé Lemire urged factory owners to provide land for their employees to grow their own vegetables. A paternalistic organization grew up that was sponsored by the Vichy government during World War II, a fact that subsequently discredited it. In any case, postwar vegetable gardening had dreary associations with penury and rationing. Ninety percent of big city allotments disappeared, in spite of their name being changed from "working-class" to "family" gardens.[102] Today there is a definite revival everywhere. They are considered to be a "green lung," "a healthy activity for retired people," and "a factor for social cohesion." In many cities, factory workers have been replaced by immigrants and the long-term unemployed.[103] The Castellas Association gets more than thirty requests for gardens every year. Its gardeners hold their title only temporarily and lose it if they neglect their plots. The public only visits on certain Garden Open days and only because publicity helps protect this exceptional heritage and ensure its survival.

From the street, it is hard to imagine the rich variety of this little garden-city spread out in nine sections. The steep hillside is terraced, each level providing splendid views of the port of Marseille. The bottom limit is clearly marked by a rail line and a major road axis—both likely to expand and reduce allotment land. The latter does not belong to the association but is owned in equal parts by a major insurance company and by the state—and the state-run railroad. The association's working income depends essentially on gardeners' subscriptions and modest subsidies from the city, departmental, and regional governments. It must cover rent, insurance, and water expenses. Rémy Spehner, the current general secretary and main

Above left:
Urban allotments, originally founded for "men only," now welcome women gardeners. The Marseille Association insists that "all types of people of all backgrounds and ethnic origins are represented here, just as in the city itself."

Above right and opposite:
The gardens of Castellas are situated between a major canal and a housing development of the same name. It is their marginal existence between city and country that makes them vulnerable to urban expansion. Here, the hilltop behind hides the canal.

spokesman, came here from Alsace, bringing with him years of experience in the important complex of family gardens in eastern France. At his initiative, the association now publishes a newsletter called *The Cabbage Leaf*. They organize competitions to help gardeners get acquainted and participate in the upkeep of common paths and fences. They also drew up an inventory of some 1,500 trees and shrubs on this hillside, all maintained year round at no cost to the city. The plots themselves help preserve heirloom varieties and provide a valuable firebreak. The association is working hard to gain recognition by the city administration for all these contributions.

It has been said that home vegetable growers aim for flavor, farmers want productivity, while urban allotments gardeners prize neatness above all. Rémy Spehner observes that at the Castella, "everything must be spic-and-span." His association has been campaigning, however, for composting and mulching, hoping to break down the old-fashioned association between bare earth and tidiness. Another sign of changing times: Few of these gardeners are hunters. Most mind the weekend invasion of their otherwise peaceful space, and some complain of finding their eggplants full of lead. Yet another innovation is the presence of women gardeners.[104] Cécile Berthoux, a garden professional, is the first woman titleholder (other than widows of existing members). Old-time gardeners are still afraid that women will not work hard and be content with the merely decorative—though in

Notes : [102] *See Françoise Dubost, Op. Cit., but also Béatrice Cabedoce, Cent ans d'histoire des Jardins ouvriers 1896-1996 (Ligue française du coin de terre et du foyer, 1996), and Louisa Jones,* Kitchen Gardens of France *(Thames & Hudson, 1996).* [103] *Quotations taken from the information supplied for the Open Days of 2004, the newsletter* La Feuille de Chou *and interviews with Mr. Spehner.* [104] *The womens' equivalent was the grandmother's garden, see Nicole Arboireau,* Jardins de grands-mères *(Édisud, 1998).* [105] *See Françoise Dubost, op. cit. and* Témoignages des écrivains paysans *(Association internationale des écrivains paysans, 1992).* [106] *Christian Tamisier, "Le paysage marseillais," contribution for the COST C11 Green structure and urban planning, Marseille seminar held 20 and 21 May 2001.*

Above, left to right:
The Castellas allotments impose a standard model toolshed, but each gardener covers it differently with paint, fencing, or trellising. These huts perpetuate the Marseille custom of the weekend *cabane* on the edge of town, a folk tradition "both urban and rural, Provençal and Mediterranean," says sociologist Christian Tamisier. As in those old suburban plots, gardeners at Castellas mix vegetables, herbs, flowers, and fruit—especially a forgotten grapevine variety with fruit nicknamed "cat cojones."

rural areas, vegetable growing is almost entirely women's work![105] As for children, Cécile Berthoux first found out about the Castellas as a schoolgirl during a class visit, and groups from schools are visiting more and more frequently. Some gardeners today have even set aside a plot for their children to plant; others keep a patch of lawn with a swing in one corner. One man remembers how as a boy he had to help his parents garden after school, a heavy chore but necessary in a poor family. Now, he welcomes his grandchildren, who come to watch the butterflies (very numerous at the Castellas). The biggest change today is perhaps a new interest in teaching and sharing. Many gardeners want to hand on their hard-acquired skills and lore, as well as the heritage of the site itself. On certain occasions, they participate with other associations to set up workshops and training sessions for the public.

Christian Tamisier, a native son and a sociologist specializing in landscape history, has been promoting and defending the Castellas allotments for many years.[106] He considers that the northern working-class movement was a byproduct of an industrial revolution that never really happened in the south. Marseille allotments embody a continuity between country and town unknown in the industrial north. The Castellas gardens are a precious vestige of this special regional heritage. But today they are also a place for "relaxing, sharing, learning, meeting, and exchanging with other people."

Ambulo, Ergo Sum...

Andy Goldsworthy at Digne

Area: The geological reserve is 734 square miles; Goldsworthy's Art Refuges are
scattered along a hiking trail about 8 miles long. Creators: Andy Goldsworthy
and others, including herman de vries; Erik Samakh, Henri Olivier, Agathe Larpent,
Jean-Simon Pagès, (director of the Geological Reserve), Nadine Gomez, (curator of
the Gassendi Museum). Musée Gassendi begun in 1889, renovated in 2002; outdoor
sculpture museum begun in 1985; Goldsworthy's participation as of 1995; first
Art Refuge in 1999.

_____ "*Ambulo, ergo sum*" (I walk, therefore I am).
Such was the answer given to Descartes by seventeenth-
century Provençal scholar Pierre Gassendi, whose name
now graces the town museum at Digne-les-Bains in the
Alpes-de-Haute-Provence.[107] The museum has become
the starting point for a vast Land Art trail through the local
geological reserve (labeled "European geopark" by Unesco).

Notes : [107] *A phrase taken up by artist herman de vries; see the exhibition catalogue available from the Réunion des musées nationaux:
ReConnaître: les choses mêmes, herman de vries, extrait du journal de Digne (Réserve géologique de Haute-Provence
and the Departmental Museum of Digne).*

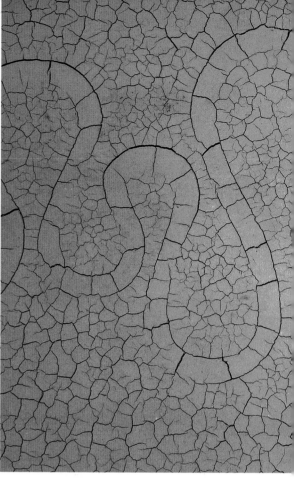

Thanks to this major project linking nature discovery and contemporary art, the region can now boast sculpture by major international artists, including the world's largest collection of works by British artist Andy Goldsworthy.

The people who began this venture wanted to revive a remote rural region through a carefully conceived version of green tourism. Guy Martini, founder of the reserve, valued from the outset "the economic and touristic potential of the area's rich geological heritage," without forgetting the "sustainability of the territory's way of life and of its inhabitants.[108] Andy Goldsworthy first came here in 1995 for a temporary exhibit but subsequently developed the idea of the Art Refuges now under construction. Accessible only on foot, these drystone remnants of rural history— a chapel, a sheepfold—have been converted by the artist into shelters for hikers. In them, architecture, sculpture, and nature coalesce.

The Gassendi Museum was founded by nineteenth-century Provençal landscape painter and poet Étienne Martin. His works are hung with other nineteenth-century landscapes in the very gallery where one end wall has been converted into Goldsworthy's famous serpentine clay work *Earth River*, photographed for the cover of his book, *Time*.[109] From Gassendi through Etienne Martin to Goldworthy, the time trail reveals our changing attitudes and experiences of the natural world from the Renaissance onward. Leaving the museum, visitors then discover the Open Air Promenade overlooking the town and

Notes : [108] *Material was taken from the following websites: Réserve Géologique de Haute-Provence, Réserve Naturelle Nationale* http://www.resgeol04.org/; www.bureaudescompetences.org/gold3.html *(now expired) which published the text "The Art Refuges, Declaration of Intention by theArtist" from June 1999 (text reprinted, it is to be hoped, on the new site* www.musee-gassendi.org)*; and finally the very interesting site* www.eyestorm.com/artists/, *which published excerpts from Goldsworthy's diaries of 1995. See also the following books:* Hand to Earth: Andy Goldsworthy Sculpture 1976–1990 *(Abrams, 1990); Gilles A. Tiberghien,* Nature, Art, Paysage *(Actes Sud, 2001); and especially Andy Goldsworthy,* Varia: Refuges d'Art, *with an audio CD interview with Goldsworthy (Editions Artha, available from the Museum in Digne).*

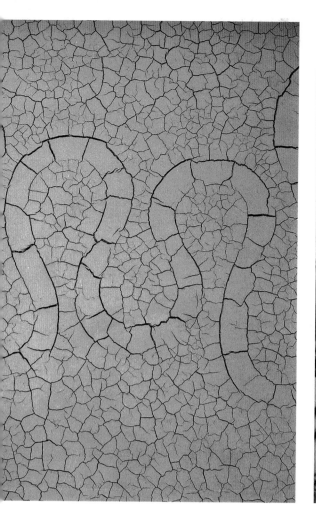

Above from
left to right:
A gallery at the Musée Gassendi
exhibits nineteenth-century
Provençal landscape paintings
surrounding Andy Goldsworthy's
"Earth River;" close-up of the clay
mural "Earth River;" Goldsworthy
working in one of the nine Art
Refuges. The artist, who is himself
a photographer, documents his
own work as it progresses.

Notes : [109] *On the cover of*
Time *(Thames & Hudson, 2000).*
[110] *Andy Goldsworthy,* op. cit.

the river Bléone. Three paths on its hillside link various outdoor artworks celebrating running water. Goldsworthy contributed here five massive stone cairns built over a hidden stream. A second museum built high on ancient ramparts perpetuates landscape memory, while providing exhibit space for temporary artists in residence.

From here, visitors can set out to discover Goldsworthy's three "sentinels," stone cones which stand at the entrance to each of three valleys in the natural park. The Art Refuges complete the series. Curator Nadine Gomez, a key figure in this project, says it takes about twelve days to explore them seriously. She points out that only one French person in three goes to museums whereas nearly 70 percent of the population goes hiking: "Walking is a kind of initiation, a way of taking distance from everyday life, of experiencing natural space in this mountain region. It is a homage to slowing down, to deep breathing, to silence."

Why would an artist as famous as Goldsworthy accept financial sacrifices to work in these hidden valleys? In the original project statement of June 1999, he explained that "this project fits extremely well into my own need for having a strong and deep relationship with particular places. Digne has more than proved itself in its ability to provide me with an extraordinarily rich context for my work"[112] His materials here are earth, stone, water, forest, and weather. The reserve pushes site memory back three million years, including two thousand years of human habitation. Goldsworthy sees his art as a layer

of human experience added to what went before. He experiences here a flow of energy that links whole epochs in the same way that his own works, often produced in series, grow "naturally" out of the ones before.

Not far from Digne, Provençal writer Jean Giono also celebrated the dynamic natural flux of a mountain landscape intermingling farmland, pastures, and wilderness. Like Goldsworthy, Giono rejected the painterly Picturesque as well as the "merely" decorative vision so often associated with gardening. But Giono's "Song of the World" was sung in an antique, heroic mode. Goldsworthy avoids pastoral idealizing, even the romantic entropy of the original American Land Art. As he says, "I am not attracted to work with the extraordinary, although I appreciate and enjoy it. I am much happier working with those things considered ordinary, with the extraordinary within those." At Digne, he has found a rural population resembling his neighbors in Scotland, and like them, he works the earth daily with his bare hands. He is not proposing a new vision of "Nature"—scientific, artistic, much less touristic—but a kind of fusion with the landscape. Gardeners can identify with his desire to experience that "flux of renewal" which moves with the energy of an emerging seed.

But if the artist at work experiences moments of deep and personal union with the elements, the results are offered to the observer in the immobilized form of art, either on site, in a gallery, or at a museum. The documentation of such works has been controversial, even when Goldsworthy himself photographs and notes his own progress in diaries. At Digne, he refuses to include any explanatory material on the spot because he feels it would interfere with the visitor's immediate experience of place, which should be gripping, even visceral. The Art Refuges are special in this respect, since some even offer possibilities for sleeping! The artist explains that waking up inside a sculpture creates a new sense of intimacy with the work, the difference between mere looking and real participation.[111]

Creators of public parks and gardens are well aware of the difficulties involved in communicating private artistic experience to the public. On-site explanatory displays may impose distance, turning the work into a mere show. Perhaps the public's indirect participation should itself be somehow valued, not as secondary or derivative but worthwhile in its own right? The medieval troubadors considered that love helped lovers discover both themselves and the world, themselves *in* the world. But these poems often include a third character whose function is to bear witness. Perhaps at Digne-les-Bains, where so many talented artists have experienced fusion with the land, this witness role can fall to hikers, museum curators, photographers, art critics, and other such tourists?

Opposite and above:
Two views of a work by Agathe Larpent created in 1999; *Water Flows, Stones Stand Still*. Other works at the outdoor Musée Promenade Saint Benoît were done by Erik Samakh, herman de vries, and Henri Olivier, as well as the five Water-Cairns by Goldsworthy.

Following pages:
The Art Refuge *Thermes* by Andy Goldsworthy at Digne-les-Bains in the Alps. It is a little-known fact that this remote region possesses the largest collection in the world of the British artist's work.

Notes: [111] *Andy Goldsworthy*, op. cit.

Addresses for gardens and landscapes in Provence

Space allows for inclusion here mainly of people consulted in the making of this book. A much longer and regularly updated version of this list is available on the author's website; *www.gardeninprovence.com/louisajones/*, which also includes information on "Garden Week in Provence," organized every year in the third week in April by Louisa Jones and Bernard Dupont, in partnership with the Mirande Hotel in Avignon.

For anyone dialing from outside France, the country code 33 must be added to any French phone or FAX number, and the first 0 removed.

Other sites that provide long lists of garden references and related information are: *www.aspeco.net* (association of nursery plant collectors in France); *www.plantesdusud.com* (long lists of gardens to visit, nurseries etc.); *www.ecoforum-paca.org* (list of 118 associations); *www.cr-paca.fr* (site for the Provence-Côte d'Azur region); *www.jardinons.com* and *http://jardinons.com/reseaumedit* (two sites on shared and collective gardens, rich with all sorts of information); *www.gazettedesgardens.com* (*La Gazette des Gardens*, only current garden magazine based in the south); *www.tela-botanica.org* (network of francophone botanists); www.afidol.org/ (everything about olives); *www.ijardins.com* for general information on French gardens.

• Garden-makers of all kinds: gardenists, garden designers, landscape architects, garden planners, nurseries, land artists, and garden consultants

AGENCE-PAYSAGES Sébastien Giorgis: *landscape architect*
12, rue du Général-Grenier 84000 Avignon
Tel: 04 90 14 42 90 Fax: 04 90 14 42 98
Email address:contact@agence-paysages.fr
Website: www.agence-paysages.fr

ALEP-PAYSAGES Philippe Deliau et Juliette Hafteck: *landscape architects (Garden 12)*
Atelier Lieux et Paysages, La Glaneuse, avenue Philippe-de-Girard, 84160 Cadenet
Tel: 04 90 68 88 84 Fax: 04 90 68 88 85
Email address: contact@Alep-paysage.com
Website: www.alep-paysage.com

APPY Jean-Claude: *southern plants (Garden 8)*
Quartier Saint-Andrieux, Roussillon, 84220 Gordes
Tel: 04 90 05 62 94 Fax: 04 90 05 73 67 Email address: appy.jean-claude@wanadoo.fr

ATELIER PAYSAGES Sylvie Bruguier, Floren Bregeon: *consulting, conception, implementation and restoration*
68, boulevard Camille-Pelletan, 84400 Apt
Tel/Fax: 04 90 74 68 87
Email address: lepavillon2@wanadoo.fr

BASSON James: *garden designer*
Le Mas de la Fee, Chemin du Terray,
Le Bar sur Loup, 06620
Tel-Fax: 04 93 42 96 23
Email address: james@scapedesign.com
Website: www.scapedesign.com

BAUD Pierre: *heirloom fruit varieties, 150 varieties of fig (Garden 18)*
Le Palis, 84110 Vaison-la-Romaine
Tel.: 04 90 36 08 46 Fax: 04 90 28 71 25
Email address: pepinieres@fig-baud.com

BENECH Louis: *landscape architect (chapter IV)*
4, cité Saint-Chaumont, 75019 Paris
Tel.: 01 42 01 04 00 Fax: 01 42 01 01 05
Email address: louis@lbenech.com

BERTHOUX Cécile: *urbanist, gardener in the allotment gardens of Marseille (Garden 29)*
chez Lire la Ville, 10, rue Colbert, 13001 Marseille
Tel.: 04 91 91 40 61
Email address: cecileberthoux@hotmail.com

BIEHN Michel: *"House and garden magic" (Gardens 8 and 15)*
7, avenue Quatre-Otages, 84800 Isle-sur-la-Sorgue
Tel.: 04 90 20 89 04 Fax: 04 90 38 45 09
Email address: lamaisonbiehn@wanadoo.fr

BORJA Erik: *designer of Zen gardens (chapter III and Garden 18)*
Les Clermonts, 26600 Beaumont-Monteux
Tel/Fax: 04 75 07 32 27

BOSC Hugues: *architect (Gardens 6 and 17)*
38, boulevard Victor-Hugo BP 29,
13532 Saint-Rémy-de-Provence
Tel: 04 90 92 10 81 Fax: 04 90 92 38 05
Email address: Bosc.architecte@wanadoo.fr

BOURDEAU Benoît: *gardenist, former head gardener of Serre de la Madone*
Villa Lotus Bleu, 4 chemin du Peyronnet, 06500 Menton
Tel/Fax: 04 93 41 48 03
Email address: benoitbourdeau@conseil.org
Website: www.benoitbourdeau.fr

BRAUN Nurseries: *climbers, Mediterranean and subtropical species (Garden 27)*
Pierre and Pia Braun, 1016, route de Saint-Rémy,
13630 Eyragues
Tel/Fax: 04 90 92 89 56
Email address: pepbraun@aol.com

BROOKES John: *Landscape architect*
(*chapter 1 + Garden 9*)
Clock House, Denmans, Fontwell, West Sussex,
BN18 0SU, England
Tel: 01243 542808. Fax: 01243 544064.
Email address: denmans@denmans-garden.co.uk

CABINET D'AGRONOMIE PROVENÇALE
(*Garden 13*) Consultation, conception and maintenance
of vineyards, olive orchards and truffle plantations
Contact: Laurence Berlemont,
349, avenue de Lattre-de-Tassigny, BP 17, 83170 Brignoles
Tel: 04 94 59 12 96 Fax: 04 94 59 16 11
Email address: cabagronomie@wanadoo.fr

CAO Angel: *gardenist-designer-nurseryman*
specializing in Spanish plants (*Garden 16*)
La Réglisserie, route nationale 106, 30190 Moussac
Tel/Fax: 04 66 81 77 14
Email address: masdelagave.@wanadoo.fr

CLÉMENT Gilles: *landscape architect,*
novelist, philosopher, artist
Atelier Acanthe, 213,
rue du Faubourg-Saint-Antoine, 75011 Paris
Tel: 01 43 48 61 33 Fax: 01 43 48 93 23
Website: www.gillesclement.com

CNUDDE Sandrine: *landscape architect* (*Garden 16*)
Terre d'Ombre, 3, rue Saint-Romain, 30700 Uzès
Tel: 04 66 03 44 48
Email address: sandrine_cnudde@yahoo.fr

COLLADO Bruno: *designer-gardenist* (*Garden 25*)
1394, chemin de la Lègue, 84200 Carpentras
Tel/Fax: 04 90 60 28 46

CRIBIER Pascal: *landscape architect* (*Garden 20*)
6, place Edmond-Rostand, 75006 Paris
Tel: 01 43 26 46 46

CUCHE Pierre and Monique: *nursery of rare*
Mediterranean plants (*Garden 9*)
Devant-Ville, 83830 Clavier
Tel/Fax: 04 94 76 63 91

DINGWALL-MAIN Alex: *landscape architect,*
author (*chapters 1 and IV*)
Landscape Enterprises,
Les Barbiers 84490 Saint Saturnin les Apt
Tel: 04 90 75 86 34 Fax: 04 90 75 88 09
Email address: enquiries@admgarden.com

DUTHOIT Rémi: *landscape architect and*
land artist (*chapter IV*)
6, rue Grobet, 13001 Marseille
Tel: 04 91 47 19 75
Website: http://remistral.free.fr

FARAGOU Alain: *landscape architect* (*Garden 4*)
Agence Faragou, 4, rue Antoine-Gautier, 06300 Nice
Tel: 04 93 55 17 55 Fax: 04 93 55 03 33
Email address: alain.faragou.paysages@wanadoo.fr
Website: www.faragou-paysages.com

FÉLIZA Jean-Laurent: *landscape architect*
(*Gardens 7 and 14*)
Agence mouvements et paysages
Les Aubépines, 10, avenue des Martyrs de la
Résistance, 83980 Le Lavandou
Tel/Fax: 04 94 71 73 43
E-mail Address: jlfelizia@free.fr
www.mouvementsetpaysages.fr

FILIPPI Clara et Olivier: *nursery for*
drought-resistant plants (*Garden 20*)
Route nationale 113, 34140 Mèze
Website: http://www.jardin-sec.com

GOLDSWORTHY Andy: *land artist* (*Garden 30*)
Galerie Lelong, 13, rue de Téhéran, 75008 Paris

GORIS Bruno: *restoration of historic*
gardens, creative design
L'Ostaou deil Bailéa, chemin du Paradis, 06620 Gourdon
Tel: 06 07 42 03 53 Fax: 04 93 42 55 17

GUIBERT Lionel: *landscape architect* (*Garden 20*)
21, rue du Faubourg-Saint-Antoine, 75011 Paris
Tel: 01 47 00 70 70
Email address: lionelguibert@9online.fr

GUILLAUMONT Natacha: *landscape architect*
(*chapter VI*)
La Compagnie du vent, 5, rue du Petit-Chantier,
13007 Marseille
Tel: 06 71 63 69 74
Email address: natacha.guillaumont@free.fr

HERVE Yves: *gardenist* (*Garden 23*)
219, avenue Brosset, 83220 Le Pradet
Tel: 04 94 75 13 41 Fax: 04 94 75 26 65

JACQUEMET Alain: *technician, gardenist,*
specialist in small gardens
Château Champlain, 84100 Orange
Tel/Fax: 04 90 34 41 80
Email address: emili.jac@tele2.fr

KROLL Simone: *vegetable gardens, low-rent*
housing projects (*chapter V*)
20, avenue Louis-Berlaimont, B-1160 Bruxelles
Tel: +32 26 73 35 39 Fax: +32 2 673 89 27
Website: http://homeusers/brutele.be/kroll

LAFOURCADE Dominique: *garden designer;*
Bruno et Alexandre Lafourcade: house restoration.
(*Gardens no. 2 and 7; chapters III and IV*)
10 boulevard Victor Hugo,
13210 Saint Rémy de Provence
Tel: 04 90 92 10 14 Fax: 04 90 92 49 72
Email address: b.lafourcade@wanadoo.fr
or laure.jakobiak@wanadoo.fr
Website www.architecture-lafourcade.com

LARPENT Agathe: *sculptor and potter* (*Garden 30*)
Le Village, 04380 Thoard
Tel/Fax: 04 92 34 61 98

MARTIN-PREVEL Benoît:
landscape architect (*Garden 22*)
Moussejonc
599 Chemin des Coussides Longues, 84150 Jonquières
Tel: 06 16 48 60 75
Email address: martin.prevel@wanadoo.fr

MARTINEZ Joël: *technician-gardener*
Les Gardens de la Carita
Route de la Carita, 13440 Cabannes
Tel/Fax: 04 90 95 37 21

MATHER Rick: *architect* (*Garden 14*)
123, Camden High Street, London NW1 7RJ, England
Tel: (44) 207 284 1727 Fax: (44) 207 267 7826
Website: www.rickmather.com

MAURIÈRES Arnaud and OSSART Éric:
landscape architects, land artists, authors (*Garden 19*)
Ossart et Maurières Sarl, 2 rue Henri Drussy, 41000 Blois
Tel: 02 54 55 06 37 Fax: 02 54 58 92 53 Email
address: ossart-maurières@wanadoo.fr
May also be contacted through David Gobaut
Tel: 06 10 24 16 90
Email address: arbressence@infonie.fr

MERLE Gilles: *Gardenist* L'Espigaou
955, chemin des Saints-Pères, 13090 Aix-en-Provence
Tel/Fax: 04 42 20 59 93

MULLER Camille: *designer* (*chapter 5*)
211, rue du Faubourg-Saint-Antoine, 75011 Paris
Tel: 01 43 67 46 95 Fax: 01 40 09 04 79

MUS Jean & Co.: *designers*
(*Garden 10 + chapter III*)
16, rue Frédéric-Mistral, BP 10, 06530 Cabris
Tel.: 04 93 60 54 50
Email address: jean.mus@wanadoo.fr
Website: www.jeanmus.com

NAVARRO François: *landscape consultant*
3, place César-Ossola, 06130 Grasse
Tel/Fax: 04 93 36 96 07
Email address: navarro.francois@club-internet.fr

NUCERA Marc: *landscape pruning, land art, design*
(pp. 13, 40, 100, 129, 131, 134, 142, 188)
4, rue du Four, BP 16, 13550 Noves
Tel/Fax: 04 90 92 99 21

PAUL Anthony: *landscape architect (Garden 25)*
Black & White Cottage, Standon Lane, Ockley Surrey,
RH5 5QR England
Tel: (44) 1306 627677 Fax: (44) 1306 627662
Email address: apaul1945@aol.com
Website: www.hannahpescharsculpture.com

PETITCOLLOT Christophe: *architect (chapter IV)*
551, chemin de Saint Arnoux, 06140 Tourrettes-sur-Loup
Tel: 04 93 59 36 66

PONCEAU Christophe: *designer-scenographer*
14, rue du Repos, 75020 Paris
Tel: 01 53 27 06 09
Website: www.ruedurepos.com

PRIVAT François: *architect (Garden 16)*
14, place Dampmartin, 30700 Uzès
Tel: 04 66 22 45 71
Email address: francois.privat@wanadoo.fr

REES Tim: *landscape architect (chapters II and IV)*
Trees Associates
30 Greenhill Park, London NW10 9AP, England
Tel: 44 (0) 208 965 7085 FAX: 44 (0) 208 838 0532
Email address: tim@treesassociates.com

RICHERT Alain: *landscape architect, artist, botanist,
author (chapter VI)*
Fax: 02 33 39 58 22

RIM, Jean-Claude: *restructuring of abandoned
gardens. (Garden 5)*
Route Pont Julien, 84480 Bonnieux
Tel: 06 07 55 54 18
Email address: j.c.rim@wanadoo.com

REY Jean-Marie: *vast nursery with many branches,
research. (Garden 3 and chapter IV)*
Head office: Gardenerey Lalonde,
Rd 559 83250 La Londe les Maures
Tel: 04 94 00 41 00 Fax: 04 94 05 23 13
Email address: Jardinerey.frejus@wanadoo.fr.

SEMINI Michel: *landscape architect
(Gardens 6 and 24)*
rue Saint-Frusquin, 84220 Goult
Tel: 04 90 72 38 50 Fax: 04 90 72 38 52

SCHREYER Jean-Louis: *gardenist-designer*
30, boulevard Mirabeau,
13210 Saint-Rémy-de-Provence
Tel/Fax: 04 32 60 03 19
Email address: jlschreyer@wanadoo.fr

SOLDI Jean-Michel: *artisan-designer (Garden 25)*
Campagne La Fenouillette, 83510 Saint-Antonin
Tel: 06 07 85 76 69

TEZE (Latour-Tézé) Ione: *designer (chapter XI)*
"Nogant," route du Pont-Julien, 84480 Bonnieux
Tel: 06 83 20 38 12
Email address: ione.teze@wanadoo.fr

RAYNAUD Jean-Louis & KRAMER Kenyon:
decoration, design (chapter XI)
3, place des Trois-Ormeaux, 13100 Aix-en-Provence
Tel: 04 42 23 52 32 Fax 04 42 23 29 07

VAN GESSEL Michael R.: *landscape architect
(Garden 1)*
Bloemgracht 40, 1015 TK Amsterdam, Holland
Tel: +31 20 625 33 69 Fax: +31 20 421 45 88
Email address: Mvangessel@cs.com

WILLIS Catherine: *sculptor in scents (chapter VI)*
64, rue Saint-Sabin, 74011 Paris
Tel: 01 43 57 16 77 ou 02 33 36 93 20
Email address: catherine@willis.ms
Website: www.catherinewillis.com

WILLS Anthony Archer:
specialist in water gardens (Garden 3)
Websites: www.archerwills.com and
www.sweetwaterdesigngroup.biz

WILMOTTE & Associés: *architects
(Gardens 10 and 20)*
68, rue du Faubourg-Saint-Antoine, 75012 Paris
Tel: 01 53 02 22 22 Fax: 01 43 44 17 11
Email address: wilmotte@wanadoo.fr

WIRTZ INTERNATIONAL SA: *landscape architects
(Garden 21)*
464 Botermelkdijk, B-2900 Schoten, Belgique
Tel: +32 3 680 13 22 Fax: +32 3 680 13 23
Email address: info@wirtznv.be
Website: www.wirtznv.be

• Associations, Schools, and Workshops; Resources
for Professionals or New Garden Owners

ALPES DE LUMIERE: *Mediterranean university for
architectural and garden heritage*
BP 58, 04301 Forcalquier Cedex
Tel: 04 92 75 22 01 Fax: 04 92 75 46 10
Email address: adl-assoc@wanadoo.fr
Website: www.alpes-de-lumiere.assoc.fr

AMIS DES PARCS ET GARDENS
MEDITERRANEENS
(Friends of Mediterranean Parks and Gardens),
(Garden 3): *courses offered by Nicole Arboireau:
historian, botanist, author*
La Pomme d'Ambre-Jardin conservatoire de la Flore
en Provence littorale Impasse ancienne route d'Italie
Tour de Mare 83600 Fréjus
Tél. : 04 94 53 25 47 Fax : 04 94 52 95 50
e.mail: nicole.arboireau@wanadoo.fr
Website: www.gardeninprovence.com/frnicole.html

APARE (Association pour la participation
de l'action régionale):
volunteer workshops for students
25, boulevard Paul-Pons, 84000 Avignon
Tel: 04 90 85 51 15 Fax: 04 90 86 82 19
Email address: apare@apare-gec.org
Website: www.apare-gec.org

ARTISTES AU JARDIN (Artists in the Garden):
seminars and exchanges (Garden 19)
Jean and Martine Deparis
Mas du Licon, 30700 Saint-Quentin-La-Poterie
Tel: 04 66 22 90 40 Fax: 04 66 22 79 34
Email address: martine.deparis@wanadoo.fr

CEEP (Conservatoire-études des écosystèmes
de Provence): *study of local ecosystems*
890, chemin de Bouenhoure haut, 13090 Aix-en-Provence
Tel: 04 42 20 03 83 Fax: 04 42 96 21 08
Email address: jc-heidet-ceep@club-internet.fr
Website: www.espaces-naturels-provence.com

LA DEMEURE HISTORIQUE (Historic Properties):
Hôtel de Nesmond, 57, quai de la Tournelle, 75005 Paris
Tel: 01 55 42 60 00 Fax: 01 43 29 36 44
Email address: contact@demeure-historique.org
Website www.demeure-historique.org

DIRECTION REGIONALE DES
AFFAIRES CULTURELLES:
Regional Administration for Historic monuments
23, boulevard du Roi-René, 13617 Aix-en-Provence Cedex
Tel: 04 42 16 19 00
Correspondent for gardens and documentarlist: Jean Marx
Tel: 04 42 16 19 29 Fax: 04 42 16 19 21
Email address: jean.marx@culture.gouv.fr

ÉCOLE NATIONALE SUPÉRIEURE DU PAYSAGE:
*southern branch of the professional school for
landscape architecture of Versaille*
Antenne Méditerranée, 10, place de la Joliette—
Les Docks Atrium 10.8
13567 Marseille Cedex 02
Tel: 04 91 91 00 25 Fax: 04 91 91 28 81
Website: www.versailles.ecole-paysage.fr

HISTORIC GARDENS FOUNDATION:
exchanges, journal, annual prizes
Gillian Mawrey 34, River Court, Upper Ground,
London SE1 9PE, England
Tel:+44 (0)20 7633 9165 Fax:+44 (0)20 7401 7072
Email address: histgard@aol.com
Website: www.historicgardens.org

HORTUS: *organizes garden seminars at the Alchemist
Gardens (Garden 19)*
Mas de la Brune, 13810 Eygalières
Tel: 04 90 90 67 77 Fax: 04 90 95 99 21
Email address: contact@jardin-alchimiste.com
Website: www.jardin-alchimiste.com

KOKOPELLI Association: *heirloom vegetable
seeds in cooperation with Seed Savers*
Head office: Oasis, 131, impasse des Palmiers, 30100 Alès
Tel: 04 66 30 00 55 Fax: 04 66 30 61 21
Email address: kokopelli.semences@wanadoo.fr
Website: www.kokopelli-seed-foundation.com

**JARDINIERS AUTOUR DE LA MÉDITERRANÉE
(JAM):** *professional association of young gardeners
working in Riviera gardens*
Head office: 47 bis, promenade Robert-Schuman,
06190 Roquebrune-Cap-Martin

LEMNA: *gardening school for owners and enthusiasts,
esthetics and culture of the Mediterranean garden
(chapter IV and Garden 30)*
Henri Olivier, Moulin de la Présa, 286, chemin de la
source, La Vernéa, 06390 Contes
Tel/Fax: 04 93 79 26 58
Email address: henriolivier@club-internet.fr

MEDITERRANEAN GARDEN SOCIETY
Western Provence and Languedoc: Jocelyn van Riemsdijk
Moulin du Gavot, Saint-Maximin, 30700 Uzès
Email address: jocelyn.vanriemsdijk@club-internet.fr
Website: www.MediterraneanGardenSociety.org

OUSTAU DE BAUMANIERE: *gardening courses
with André Gayraud in French*
13520 Les Baux-de-Provence
Tel: 04 90 54 33 07 Fax: 04 90 54 40 46
Email addresses: contact@oustaudebaumaniere.com
or contact@lacabrodor.com.
Websites: www.oustaudebaumaniere.com or
www.lacabrodor.com

**PARCS ET JARDINS DE PROVENCE-ALPES-
COTE D'AZUR:** *regional branch association of
the national Parcs et Jardins de France*
Mas de Barrelet, 13890 Mouriès
Tel/Fax: 04 90 47 50 62
Email address: paborgeap@wanadoo.fr

RARE PLANTS AND NATURAL GARDENS
BP 24, 84830 Sérignan-du-Comtat
Tel: 06 30 24 45 31
Website: www.plantes-rares.com

PRAEDIUM RUSTICUM: *associated with the national
organization Parcs et Gardens de France*
President Henri de Colbert, château de Flaugergues,
1744, avenue Einstein, 34000 Montpellier
Tel: 04 99 52 66 39 Fax: 04 99 52 66 44
Email address: praedium-amis-des-jardins@wanadoo.fr

RUE DES JARDINS: *to preserve and promote
old village gardens*
Juliette Mellet, rue Costa-Caoudo, 84160 Cucuron
Tel.: 04 90 77 28 41
Email address: juliette.mellet@freesurf.fr
or Guillaume Argentin, rue de France, 84240 Ansouis
Tel: 04 90 09 12 80

LA SAUVEGARDE DES OLIVADES: *market
gardening farm specializing in heirloom varieties,
threatened by urban renewal*
933, chemin de Fabrégas, 83500 La-Seyne-sur-Mer
Tel: 04 94 87 23 42
Email address: sauvolivades@free.fr
Website: http://fr.groups.yahoo.com/group/sauvolivades

SOCIÉTÉ CENTRALE D'AGRICULTURE,
*d'horticulture et d'acclimatation de Nice et des
Alpes-maritimes: Riviera garden association organizing
workshops and lectures*
Palais de l'Agriculture
113, Promenade des Anglais, 06200 NICE
Tel/Fax: 04 93 86 58 E-mail scanice@wanadoo.fr
Website: http://perso.wanadoo.fr/s

SOCIÉTÉ DES GENS DE GARDEN
1233, chemin des Rastines, 06600 Antibes
Tel/Fax: 04 93 65 88 47
Website: www.jardinsdusud.com

SALAGON (Prieuré de): *Musée-Conservatoire
ethnologique de Haute-Provence*
Gardens created with the help of ethnobotanist Pierre
Lieutaghi and designers Bruel-Delmar
04300 Mane
Tel: 04 92 75 70 50 Fax: 04 92 75 70 58
Email address: Musee.salagon@wanadoo.fr
Website: www.musee-de-salagon.com or www.cg04.fr

TERRE ET HUMANISME:
Founder: ecological agronomist Pierre Rabhi
Mas de Beaulieu BP 19, 07230 Lablachère
Tel: 04 75 36 64 01 Fax: 04 75 36 68 20
Website: http://terrehumanisme.free.fr/rabhi/rabhi.htm

**SOCIETE D'HORTICULTURE ET
D'ARBORICUTLURE DES BOUCHES-DU-RHONE,**
Annex of the Agricultural Lycée at Saint-Germain-en-Laye
Parc Bortoli, 2, chemin du Lancier, 13008 Marseille
Tel: 04 91 40 62 66 Fax: 04 91 40 48 45

TERRE VIVANTE: *experimental farm, workshops
on gardens and ecological living*
Terre Vivante, Domaine de Raud, 38710 Mens
Tel.: 04 76 34 80 80 Fax: 04 76 34 84 02
Email address: infos@terrevivante.org
Website: http://terrevivante.org

**VIEILLES MAISONS FRANÇAISES
(Historic Properties)**
93, rue de l'Université, 75006 Paris
Tel: 01 40 62 61 71 Fax: 01 45 51 12 26
Website: www.vmf.net

VOLUBILIS: *a link between human beings and their land*
8, rue Frédéric-Mistral, 84000 Avignon
Tel: 04 90 14 42 98 Fax: 04 90 14 42 91
Email address: a.volubilis@wanadoo.fr
Website: www.volubilis.org

DRYSTONE CONSTRUCTION (chapter 5)
See, above all, the website www.pierreseche.com,
which is full of information.

**ASPPSV (Association for the preservation of
the drystone heritage of the Var):**
Contact E. Kalmar, 8 rue Victor Maria, 83650
Les Arcs or Musée des arts et traditions populaires du Var,
rue Roumanille, 83300 Draguignan.

**ASSENEMCE (association for the preservation
of sites and environment in northeastern
Marseille and the Étoile mountains):**
*Conservatory of terraces, orchards and Mediterranean
gardens of Marseille, in process*
Relais-nature Saint-Joseph, 64, boulevard Simon-Bolivar,
13014 Marseille
Tel/Fax: 04 91 60 84 07
Email address: assenemce@free.fr
Website: www.ecoforum-paca.org

**ASSOCIATION "SUR LE SENTIER DES
LAUZES" (on the Slate Trail):**
07260 Saint-Mélany
Tel: 04 75 36 96 46
Website: www.surlesentierdeslauzes.fr

**CENTRE DE RESSOURCES SUR LES TERRASSES
(Resource Center For Terraces):**
Château de Logères, Association Fontaine de Logères
Tel: 04 75 88 39 38
Email address: logeres@free.fr

CERAV (Centre d'études régionales d'architecture vernaculaire) (vernacular architecture):
11, rue René-Villermé, 75011 Paris
Email address: cerav@pierreseche.com
Website: www.pierreseche.com/

COMMUNAUTE DE COMMUNES DE VAL DE DROME (Villages of the Drome Valley):
Terrace Conservatory Project
BP 331, 26402 Crest Jean-Noël Chamba
Tel: 04 75 25 43 82 Fax: 04 75 25 44 98

TERRACE CONSERVATORY (ADÈCHE):
The Association "Conservatoire de terrasses,"
directors Agnès Redou, Hameau de la Chareyre,
07360 St-Michel-de-Chabrillanoux
and Michel Rouvière, Le Fez, 07110 Vinézac
Tel/Fax: 04 75 36 84 77

TERRACE CONSERVATORY (VUCLUSE):
84220 Goult, at the top of the village, terraces
restored by l'APARE (q.v.), Mairie de Goult
Tel: 04 90 72 20 16 Fax: 04 90 72 28 14

LITHOS House of Drystone Construction:
(Maison de la pierre sèche Association)
Responsable Philippe Alexandre, place Albert-Morel,
84210 Le Beaucet Tel/Fax: 04 90 69 60 15
Email address: association.lithos@wanadoo.fr

TERRACE CONSERVATORY (ADECHE):
Site is part of the Parc naturel régional des monts
d'Ardèche, La Prade, 07560 Montpezat-sous-Bauzon
Tel: 04 75 94 35 20
Website: www.parc-monts-ardeche.fr
Sites à Ailhon, Joannas, Veyras, Laurac-en-Vivarais,
Saint-Mélany, Saint-Michel-de-Chabrillanoux

PARC NATUREL REGIONAL DU LUBERON:
leader of the network REPPIS (Réseau européen des
pays de la pierre sèche)
BP 122, 60, place Jean-Jaurès, 84404 Apt Cedex
Tel: 04 90 04 42 00
Email address: contact@parcduluberon.fr
Website: http://www.parcduluberon.com

• Garden Visits and Tours

"GARDEN WEEK IN PROVENCE":
Organized by Louisa Jones
Every year, in the third week of April, Louisa Jones and
Bernard Dupont organize a week of visits to the best
gardens in the region, in partnership with the Mirande
Hotel in Avignon. The week comprises seven nights and
six days of visits, including many places accessible only
through their connections. For futher information, contact
Louisa Jones at ljones@wanadoo.fr or Martin Stein,
Hôtel La Mirande, place l'Amirande, 84000 Avignon.
Tel: 04 90 14 20 20 Fax: 04 90 86 26 85
Email address: mirande@la-mirande.fr
Website: www.la-mirande.fr.

• Gardens and Landscape Sites That Are
Private or Little Known
For the famous ones not specially mentioned in this book,
see websites at the begining of this address list.

ABBAYE DE SAINT ANDRÉ: *old-fashioned country*
gardens on picturesque ruins
Roseline Bacou, abbaye Saint-André,
30400 Villeneuve-les-Avignon
Tel/Fax: 04 90 25 55 95

ALCHEMIST'S GARDENS AND BOTANICAL
GARDEN OF MAGIC PLANT: (Garden 19)
Mas de la Brune, 13810 Eygalières
Tel: 04 90 90 67 77 Fax: 04 90 95 99 21
Email address: contact@jardin-alchimiste.com
Website: www.jardin-alchimiste.com

CÉZANNE'S STUDIO: *Summer outdoor sculpture*
festival (chapter VI)
9, avenue Paul-Cézanne 13090 Aix-en-Provence
Tel: 04 42 21 06 53 Fax: 04 42 21 90 34
Email address: atelier.cezanne@wanadoo.fr
Website: www.atelier-cezanne.com

BAMBOUS DU MANDARIN NURSERY
(Mandarin's Delight): (Garden 26)
Benoît Béraud, Pont de Siagne 83440 Montauroux
Tel: 04 93 66 12 94

BAMBOUSERAIE SA: (chapter VI)
Prafrance: world famous bamboo collections, nursery
Générargues, 30140 Anduze
Tel: 04 66 61 70 47 Fax: 04 66 61 64 15
Email address: bambou@bambouseraie.fr
Website www.bambouseraie.fr

CONSERVATOIRE DE L'ESPACE LITTORAL
ET DES RIVAGES LACUSTRES Région PACA:
(chapter VI)
Many sites, wild and gardened; a small guide is available,
Bastide Beaumanoir, 3, rue Marcal-Arnaud,
13100 Aix-en-Provence
Tel: 04 42 91 64 10 Fax: 04 42 91 64 11
Email address: paca@conservatoire-du-littoral.fr
Website: www.conservatoire-du-littoral.fr

Among the most famous domains of the
Conservatoire du littoral:

Serre de la Madone (chapters II and IV)
Lawrence Johnston's Riviera garden from 1924
74, route du Val-de-Gorbio 06500 Menton
Tel: 04 93 57 73 90
Email address: Visites@serredelamadone.com
Website: www.serredelamadone.com

Domaine du Rayol, Mediterranean biomes,
designed by Gilles Clément
83820 Le Rayol-Canadel
Tel: 04 93 98 04 44
Email address: adora@wanadoo.fr
Website: www.domainedurayol.org

Domaine de Courbebaisse, public park
Le Pradet, office de tourisme
Tel: 04 94 21 71 69

ÉLIE'S GARDEN: *botanical collection by a pioneer*
eoclogist (chapter VI)
Chemin des Baumes, 83136 La Roquebrussane
Tel: 04 94 86 90 28 (garden) or 04 94 86 84 23
Website link www.mouvementsetpaysages.fr

GARDEN CONSERVATION OF PLANTS
FOR DYEING: (chapter 6)
Association Couleur Garance, Michel Garcia
Le Château, 84360 Lauris
Tel/Fax: 04 90 08 40 48

GERBAUD CAMPAGNE: *herb lore and*
culture in both senses
Paula Chauvin, 84160 Lourmarin
Tel.: 04 90 68 11 83 Fax: 04 90 68 37 12
Email address: cgerbaud@aol.com

GRAVESON: *garden community* (Garden 28)

Town representative: Claire Villero
Tourist office: Hôtel de Ville, Cours national,
13690 Graveson
Tel: 04 90 95 71 05 Fax: 04 90 95 81 75
Email address: ot.graveson@visitprovence.com

Garden of the Four Seasons
Avenue de Verdun
Tel: 04 90 95 88 44
Water Gardens ("Aux fleurs de l'eau"), Alain Stroppiana
Quartier Cassoulen, route de Saint-Rémy,
13690 Graveson
Tel: 04 90 95 85 02

Perfume Museum and herb garden
La Chevêche, Petite route du Grès
Tel: 04 90 958 158 Fax: 04 90 90 50 78
Email address: aromatherapy@nellygrosjean.com

Fig Farm, Francis and Jacqueline Honoré
Mas de Luquet, 13690 Graveson
Tel: 04 90 95 72 03 Fax: 04 90 95 76 23
Email address: infos@lesfiguieres.com
Website: www.lesfiguieres.com

JARDIN DES FLEURS DE POTERIE:
open April–October, Sundays
Anne-Marie Deloire, 250, chemin des Espeiroures,
06510 Gattières
Tel/Fax: 04 93 08 67 77
Email address: jardindepoterie@mac.com
Website: http://homepage.mac.com/jardindepoterie/

JARDIN DES SAMBUCS:
Agnès and Nicholas Brückin
Le Villaret, 30570 St André de Majencoules
Tel: 04 67 82 46 47
Email address: jardinsambucs@msn.com

JARDIN ROMAIN: created by l'Agence Paysage
Chemin de la chapelle, 84510, Caumont-sur-Durance
Tel: 04 90 01 20 20

LANDSCAPE PARK FERNAND BRAUDEL: *by landscape architect Alain Faragou (Garden 4 and chapter IV)*
avenue Jean-Baptiste Mattéi, quartier des Sablettes,
83500 La Seyne-sur-Mer
Tel: 04 94 10 47 30

LAVENDER ROADS OF PROVENCE:
itineraries, contacts, information
2, avenue de Venterol, 26110 Nyons
Tel: 04 75 26 65 91 Fax: 04 75 26 32 67
Email address: info@routes-lavande.com
Website: www.routes-lavande.com/

MAISON DE LA TRUFFE ET DU VIN DU LUBERON:
garden made by Michel Biehn (Gardens 8 and 15)
Director, Nicole Guillot, place de l'Horloge, 84560
Ménerbes
Tel: 04 90 72 52 10 Fax: 04 90 72 52 15
Email address: truffeetvin@wanadoo.fr
Website: www.vin-truffe-luberon

MÉMOIRE DE GARRIGUE: *landscape history
trail next to the famous Roman aquaduct, the
Pont du Gard (chapter 6)*
BP7 30210 Vers-Pont-du-Gard
Tel: 08 20 90 33 30 Fax: 04 66 37 51 50
Website: www.pontdugard.fr

MUSÉE GASSENDI: *(Garden 30)*
Curator: Nadine Gomez-Passamar
64, boulevard Gassendi, 04000 Digne-les-Bains
Tel: 04 92 31 45 29 Fax: 04 92 32 38 64
Website: www.musee-gassendi.org

Musée-promenade Saint-Benoît:
Natural Geological Reserve of Haute-Provence
Director, Jean-Simon Pagès
04000 Digne
Tel: 04 92 36 70 70
Website: http://www.resgeol04.org/

**Hiking Tours of Goldsworthy's Art Refuges
with mountain guides:**
Association Empreinte
Joël Marteau, Le Village, 04420 Beaujeu
Tel: 04 92 34 91 20

NATURAL REGIONAL PARK OF CAMARGUE:
Gael Hemery, commissioner for natural landscapes
Tel: 04 90 97 19 22 Fax: 04 90 97 12 07
Email address: espaces.naturels@parc-camargue.fr

LES OLIVADES: *choice tomato production and
conservation association*
Daniel and Denise Vuillon
257, chemin de la Petite-Garenne, 83190 Ollioules
Tel: 04 94 30 03 13
Email address: vuillon@olivades.com and
sauvolivades@free.fr. Website: www.olivades.com

PAVILLON DE GALON: *eighteenth-century water
garden, cooking classes*
84160 Cucuron
Tel: 04 90 77 24 15 Fax: 04 90 77 12 55
Email address: bibi@pavillondegalon.com
Website: www.pavillondegalon.com

LA POMME D'AMBRE: Garden for the
Preservation of Coastal Species Nicole Arboireau:
historian, botanist, author
Impasse ancienne route d'Italie Tour de Mare
83600 Fréjus
Tél.: 04 94 53 25 47 Fax: 04 94 52 95 50
Email address: nicole.arboireau@wanadoo.fr
Website: www.gardeninprovence.com/frnicole.html

**REST AREA ON MOTORWAY
NÎMES-CAISSARGUES** *(chapter VI):* the work of
famous architect Bernard Lassus, on the A55, between
Nîmes and the airport Nîmes-Garons, accessible in
both directions.

VAL JOANIS CHÂTEAU:
winery, terraced potager
84120 Pertuis
Tel: 04 90 79 20 77
Website: www.val-joanis.com

VALLON DU VILLARET:
nature discovery park with land art
48190 Bagnols-les-Bains
Tel: 04 66 47 63 76 Fax: 04 66 47 63 83
Email address: vallon@levillaret.fr
Website: www.levillaret.fr

VILLA NOAILLES: *Parc Saint-Bernard.* Curator of
collections, Pierre Quillier *(Garden 28 and chapter V)*
Montée de Noailles, 83400 Hyères
Service espaces verts
Tel: 04 94 00 78 65

**• Gardens Open By Appointment
For Occasional Visits Only**
*Many of these can be visited during the Open Gardens
(Journées du patrimoine) weekend held in June and
September, or for special events.*

BRANTES (château): *historic garden with
recent creations by Semini and Benech*
83700 Sorgues
Tel: 04 90 39 11 73 Fax: 04 90 39 23 36
Email address: ch2b@wanadoo.fr
Website: www.jardinez.com/jardindebrantes

LA CHABAUDE: *designers Vésian, Idoux
(chapter IV and Gardens 5, 17 and 18)*
and recently Cottet Owner Scott Stover
Email address: cottet.philippe@wanadoo.fr

LA CHÈVRE D'OR: *famous postwar garden
lovingly maintained (Garden 23)*
Fax: 00 31 705 11 43 60
Email address: visites@lachevredor.com
Website: www.lachevredor.com

CLOS DU PEYRONET: *historic and botanical garden*
William Waterfield, avenue Aristide-Briand, 06500 Menton
Tel: 04 93 35 72 15

DESCRIER, Nicole: Near Grasse
Email address: felbert@wanadoo.fr

DOMAINE DU PRIEURE, Joanna Millar:
terraced plant collections
106, route de Courmettes, 06140 Tourette-sur-Loup
Fax: 04 93 59 36 39
Email address: milljo@wanadoo.fr

LA GRANDE BASTIDE: *historic property and arboretum*
Françoise Desnuelle-d'Anselme de Puisaye, 84220 Goult
Tel: 04 90 72 37 27
Email address: desnuelle@wanadoo.fr
GARDEN OF THE ANTIPODES:
inspired by New Zealand forests. No groups.
Alexandra Boyle, 87 bd de Garavan, 06500 Menton
Fax: 04 93 35 64 42
Email address: AlexBoyle43@hotmail.com

TROPICAL GARDEN OF MENTON: collector's
garden near the beach
Jean Gatumel, 47 bis, promenade Robert-Schuman
06190 Roquebrune-Cap Martin

ALLOTMENT GARDENS OF MARSEILLE,
"Le Castellas": (Garden 29)
Secrétaire: Rémy Spehner, BP 29,
13314 Marseille Cedex 15
Chemin de Saint-Antoine à Saint-Joseph, Marseille
(15e) Entrance at the level of no. 59, opposite the
pharmacy. By bus: no.31, bus stop "Le Castellas"
Tel: 04 91 08 24 15 or 04 91 08 91 13

JURION Roland: mountain botanical garden,
small groups only
La Jasminade, 110, chemin des Bergeronnettes
06620 Le Bar-sur-Loup
Tel: 04 93 42 70 30

LA LOUVE: garden created by Nicole de Vésian
(Garden 5 and chapters I and IV)
Owner: Judith Pillsbury 84480 Bonnieux
Email address: Jinfrance@aol.com

MAS de PAYAN: young botanical garden,
arboretum, potager
Route de Fontvieille 13150 Tarascon
Tel: 04 90 54 62 38
Email address: sbrignac@club-internet.fr

MÈRE VEILLEUSE (Gardens of the): imaginative
grandmother's garden (chapter I)
84570 Blauvac
Tel: 04 90 61 87 45

NOGANT: vast personal garden (chapter II)
Ione Latour-Tézé, route du Pont-Julien, 84480 Bonnieux
Tel: 04 90 75 84 77 Fax: 04 90 75 94 85
Email address: ione.teze@wanadoo.fr

LA NORIA (Garden 19)
Jean and Martine Deparis, mas de Licon,
30700 Saint-Quentin-la-Poterie
Tel: 04 66 22 90 40 Fax: 04 66 22 79 34
Email address: martine.deparis@wanadoo.fr

ROMEGAS (domaine de): historic bastide garden
Marie-Ange Rater 3912, chemin Saint-Donat,
13100 Aix-en-Provence
Tel: 04 42 23 17 53 Fax: 04 42 96 95 37
Email address: marieangerater@aol.com

STEAD, M and Mrs. Martin Stead: area of Grasse
Tel: 04 93 77 77 09

VALLON RAGET: (chapter II)
Nicole and Jacques Martin-Raget, Chemin Notre Dame
du Château, 13103 St Etienne du Grès
Tel/FAX 04 90 49 15 05.

VIGNAL (château): garden and olive oil production
Pierre and Henriette Chiesa-Gautier-Vignal
2566, route de Berre-des-Alpes, 06390 Contes
Tel: 04 93 79 00 11 Fax: 04 93 79 19 90

VILLA ORVES: (Garden 28)
Françoise Deval-Darlington, 83160 La Valette-du-Var
Tel: 04 94 20 53 25
Email address: FDarlington@compuserve.com

WEIS Denis and Marie-Françoise: (Garden 3)
Chemin du Piouret, quartier Saint-Esprit,
83830 Figanières
Tel: 04 94 67 82 76

• Bed-and-Breakfasts, Seasonal Rentals, or
Hotels with Gardens
These gardens are open only to tourists for specially
advertised events.

LES ATELIERS DE L'IMAGE: garden by
Jean-Louis Schreyer
36, boulevard Victor-Hugo,
13210 Saint-Rémy-de-Provence
Tel: 04 90 92 51 50 Fax: 04 90 92 43 52
Email address: info@hotelphoto.com

BASTIDE DE SAINT-ANTOINE: domain of two-star
chef Jacques Chibois
48, avenue Henri-Dunant, 06130 Grasse
Tel: 04 93 70 94 94 Fax: 04 93 70 94 95
Email address: info@jacques-chibois.com
Website: http://www.jacques-chibois.com/fr/sommaire.htm

BASTIDE ROSE with the Pierre Salinger
Memorial Museum: summer sculpture exhibits Poppy
Nicole Salinger and her son, Emmanuel de Menthon
99, chemin des Croupières, 84250 Le Thor
Tel: 04 90 02 14 33 Fax: 04 90 02 19 38
Email address: poppynicole@yahoo.com
Websites: www.bastiderose.com and for the
Poppy and Pierre Salinger Foundation:
www.poppyandpierresalingerfoundation.org

BEAUMONT DU VENTOUX: (Garden 1)
Contact and information: Arjan Schipper
Email address: info@webeaumont.com

DOMAINE DE LA VERRIERE: (Garden 22)
rentals for special events, professional seminars;
winery and olive oil production
84110 Crestet
Tel: 06 22 03 31 15
Email address: nicole@laverriere.com
Website: www.laverriere.com

FONTAINE-DE-FAUCON: (Garden 5)
Chemin de la Fontaine-de-Faucon,
Quartier Sainte-Anne, 84220 Goult
Tel: 04 90 72 24 96
Email address: fontainedefaucon@aol.com
Website: www.fontainedefaucon.com

HÔTEL HI: Gardens by Benoît Bourdeau
3, avenue des Fleurs, 06000 Nice
Tel: 04 97 07 26 26 Fax: 04 97 07 26 27
Email: hi@hi-hotel.net Website: www.hi-hotel.net

MAS DES CÂPRIERS: garden of aromatic plants
Christine et Bernard Tixier, chemin de Raoux,
84240 Cabrières-d'Aigues
Tel/Fax: 04 90 77 69 68
Website: www.luberon-masdescapriers.com

MAS DU LICON: (Garden 19)
30700 Saint-Quentin-la-Poterie
Tel: 04 66 22 90 40 Fax: 04 66 22 79 34
Email address: martine.deparis@wanadoo.fr

MARSHALL Lydie: cooking classes at home
(chapter V)
Le Château Feodal, 5, Cour Château-Vieux
26110 Nyons
Tel: 04 75 26 45 31 Fax: 04 75 26 09 31
Email address: ciboulette@juno.com

LA MIRANDE: charming, quiet garden
in the heart of town
Place l'Amirande, 84000 Avignon
Tel: 04 90 14 20 20 Fax: 04 90 86 26 85
Email address: mirande@worldnet.net
Website: www.la-mirande.fr

PAVILLON DE GALON: eighteenth-century water
garden, cooking classes
84160 Cucuron
Tel: 04 90 77 24 15 FAX: 33 (0) 4 90 77 12 55
Email address: bibi@pavillondegalon.com
Website: www.pavillondegalon.com

ROSERAIE DE BERTY:
famous rose nursery, wild setting
Éléonore Cruse 07110 Largentière.
Tel: 04 75 88 30 56 Fax: 04 75 88 36 93
Website: www.roseraiedeberty.free.fr

Acknowledgments

Every book is a group production, but this one more than most. I must first thank all the garden owners and professionals in the region, who encouraged me from the start with a great wave of enthusiasm. Lack of space has prevented me from describing every garden visited, but all and more besides are cited in the address list at the end. The burst of garden-making in Provence is just beginning. Every week I hear about more gardens to visit, new projects on the way . . . perhaps there will be more books to come? I must also thank my talented photographer Bruno Suet, whose fresh eye particularly suits these gardens. Art director Séverine Morizet produced an original and striking design, and Sabine Kuentz, my editor at Aubanel, was constant in her kindness, patience, and intelligence. My husband was, now as always, my first and most faithful reader . . .